INFLATABLE KAYAKING

The Complete Guide

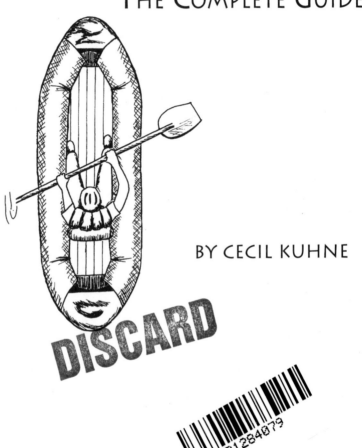

BY CECIL KUHNE

STACKPOLE BOOKS

Published by
STACKPOLE BOOKS
5067 Ritter Road
Mechanicsburg, PA 17055

Printed in the United States of America

10   9   8   7   6   5   4   3   2   1

First edition

797.1224
KUHNE
1997

Library of Congress Cataloging-in-Publication Data

Kuhne, Cecil, 1952–
    Inflatable kayaking: the complete guide / by Cecil Kuhne.
  — 1st ed.
      p.   cm.
    ISBN 0-8117-2810-2 (alk. paper)
    1. Inflatable canoes.   2. Kayaking.   I. Title.
GV790.3.K85   1997
797.1'22 — dc20   96-20666
                                                            CIP

B+H 6/3/97   15.95

To my brother Clark

INFLATABLE KAYAKING

THE COMPLETE GUIDE

An Important Note to Readers

This book contains much useful information about the sport of inflatable kayaking. Before engaging in this potentially hazardous sport, however, you must do more than read a book.

The sport requires skill, concentration, physical strength and endurance, proper equipment, knowledge of fundamental principles and techniques, and unwavering commitment to your own safety and that of your companions.

The publisher and author obviously cannot be responsible for your safety. Because inflatable kayaking entails the risk of serious and even fatal injury, we emphasize that you should not begin kayaking except under expert supervision. No book can substitute for proper training and experience under the guidance and supervision of a qualified teacher.

Introduction

The current is swift, and the paddlers work hard to reach a quiet pool along the shore, where they pull their inflatable kayaks onto the broad, sandy beach. They walk briskly through a field already trampled by those who have stopped at this very spot, and for the same reason—to take a long, close look at the rapids churning viciously below.

High above them rise snow-capped, cloud-piercing peaks. Sweeping meadows dotted with fluorescent hues of wildflowers lie below. Eagles soar quietly through the turquoise sky.

But the paddlers hardly notice. Their attention is riveted on the noise below, still blocked from sight by huge boulders scattered along the banks. They climb nervously to reach the highest vantage point. No one says a word as they peer downward into the churning mass of water roiling against rock.

Below them, the current has thrust boulders of all sizes into the river, forcing its flow against the steep cliff on the left. Though rocks have clogged the channel, the river has fingered its way through, creating chutes of various widths. But most of the passages are too narrow to be considered.

"Look at that huge hole," warns one of the kayakers as he points downstream. "But it looks like there's a tongue of water between the rocks. See it? That's where we need to be if we're going to make it."

"But the right side has a pretty steep hole," another says, trying to appear calm. "What happens if we miss and go in there?"

"Maybe we had better aim for the left side," the first kayaker replies. "The water's moving through it much better. If we flip, at least maybe we'll wash through."

The kayakers walk back to their boats and climb in for the inevitable descent. They paddle hard into the glistening current. The two huge boulders at the top of the rapids are easily located. The paddlers steer their boats between them, but the fury below is still hidden from view.

As the white froth of the rapids nears, the current swiftly pulls the inflatable kayaks downstream. For a moment, in the slack water above the rapids, the boats hang suspended. Then, with the speed of a roller coaster, the boats enter the sleek, sharply tapered tongue—a sliver of smooth, green silk unfurled before the churning whitewater. The boaters plunge downward into the watery abyss.

Like flotsam in a whirlpool, the inflatable kayaks rock from side to side as they flash past the huge swells of the cataclysm. The paddlers are drenched by its wall of water, as they stroke furiously to keep from being washed into the rocky depths.

The remaining seconds seem like hours. Amazingly enough, the kayakers come out of the intense pounding unscathed. Only a couple of hats and pairs of sunglasses have been washed overboard. The gray clouds hanging overhead have disappeared, giving way to bright, illuminating sunshine. The kayakers scream with joy at their success.

The beauty of this scenario is that the entire country is etched with rapids just like this—places where normally sane individuals congregate to scare themselves half to death. Whitewater, it seems, has this irresistible, but contradictory, effect.

At the same time that it stirs the senses, it stills the soul.

1

Why the Inflatable Kayak?

It wasn't long ago that the inflatable kayak was derided as little more than an overgrown beach toy. No one is laughing now.

The sophistication of design, materials, and manufacturing techniques has made the inflatable kayak a whitewater boat to be reckoned with. Even the normally staunch hardshell kayakers have begun to sit up and take notice. Inflatable kayaks offer a number of advantages: They're lightweight, they're relatively inexpensive, they're easy to learn to use, and they're undeniably participatory.

The inflatable kayak, often called an IK for short, is a small boat, typically about 3 feet wide and from 8 to 14 feet in length. They usually weigh 35 or 40 pounds. They're made of a variety of fabrics, usually polyester or nylon coated with synthetic rubber for durability.

The typical IK has two inflatable side tubes that form the hull of the boat. These tubes narrow to a point at the bow and stern, where the tips are joined and reinforced for added strength in the better models. A seat of some kind is usually added to provide back support for the paddler and to serve as a stiffener to keep the tubes from folding inward. Many boats now have self-bailing floors.

*The inflatable kayak is a
deceptively sophisticated
craft.* CECIL KUHNE

But is the boat a kayak or a canoe? Unlike traditional hardshell kayaks, most inflatable kayaks are not decked across the top to keep out spray. Like a canoe, the IK has a more open cockpit, allowing the paddler to easily get in and out of the boat. A hardshell kayak is designed to hold the paddler inside the boat, even when the boat turns upside down. That's why the maneuver to upright the hardshell kayak, called the Eskimo roll, must be learned early, especially when running whitewater. But with an inflatable kayak, no such skills are necessary. If you fall out, you just climb back in and start paddling again.

Like hardshell kayakers, inflatable kayakers typically use double-bladed kayak paddles, whereas canoeists use single-bladed, T-grip paddles. In a canoe, when balance is important, as in running whitewater, paddlers often kneel in their boats. Both hardshell and inflatable kayakers, on the other hand, usually sit down with their legs forward.

Hardshell boats generate less friction against the water's surface and therefore handle better than most inflatables, though this is rapidly changing with the increased rigidity of IKs. Rigid kayaks are less forgiving for beginners, however, and it takes more time to master the necessary skills.

The inflatable kayak also has certain advantages over larger inflatables. The IK puts you close to the water, offering a dramatic sense of perspective. The small rapids that looked like nothing from shore loom ahead when paddling them in an inflatable kayak. You don't have to travel far with an IK; those small local streams will prove challenging enough.

Inflatable kayaks are more prone to overturning in heavy water than large rafts, but IKs are also more maneuverable, and therefore paddlers are better able to avoid the worst holes in the river. Experienced paddlers with good-quality equipment are now running the most challenging whitewater in the world.

Low water is seldom a problem for inflatable kayaks. These boats are often the only ones capable of navigating low flows, allowing for a longer season. The inflatable kayaker, too, can paddle popular rivers outside the period that governmental permits are required to run the river. Across the country there are countless streams too small to be of interest to other boaters. This allows the inflatable kayaker a wider choice of possibilities and the opportunity to avoid the crowds.

Inflatable kayaks are lightweight and easy to handle alone. There is no pressure to run whitewater beyond your ability when it's easy to carry your boat around the rapids. On long portages, you can deflate the boat, roll it up, carry it around an obstacle, then pump it back up and you're back on the water. Compared with other whitewater craft, inflatable kayaks are easy to rig: no frames, no extensive strap system, no flotation bags.

The inflatable kayak is the perfect wilderness craft. You're comfortably sitting down, with your back braced against a padded seat and your gear piled behind for a week-long expedition. The river does most of the work, and there's plenty of room for hearty meals and other luxuries left behind on backpack trips.

Transportation of the boat is easy as well, since everything can fit into the smallest of cars. Some boaters even use public transportation to run their shuttles. You can paddle exotic locations without shipping problems, and if you really want to get away from it all, you can pack one into a bush plane or on the back of a horse. For apartment dwellers, these boats are perfect; even the largest IK will roll into a package small enough to stow under the bed or in a closet.

If you're now convinced, like many of us, that the inflatable kayak is the finest solo whitewater boat on the face of the earth, then read on, grab a paddle, and go forth!

2

THE BOAT

No one knows for sure when it all started, but the idea of inflatable boats has been around for a long time. The modern inflatable kayak dates back to World War II, when the assault raft was developed by the navy to storm the islands of the Pacific. These big, black neoprene rafts, known as "ten-mans," were manufactured by the thousands. They were later sold as surplus, and it wasn't long before they were running rivers throughout the country.

The inflatable was a tremendous advance over the hardshell boats first used to float rivers. It was cheaper and lighter, but most important, its incredible flotation and ability to bounce off rocks made it safer than any hardshell boat ever could be.

DESIGN
The early version of the inflatable kayak looked like a huge banana, bright yellow and curved to a point at each end. This was the Tahiti, developed in 1963 and mass produced by the Sevylor Corporation. Despite its limitations, this boat has been paddled on rivers throughout the world, even the Colorado River through the Grand Canyon. The Tahiti's greatest advantage was price, and they are still available at discount stores for under $150.

The Tahiti was the first inflatable kayak to be mass-produced. COURTESY OF THE SEVYLOR CORP.

Huge refinements in design, materials, and manufacturing techniques have been made since the Tahiti, however, and the number of inflatable kayak manufacturers has grown in recent years.

Today's inflatable kayak is light-years ahead of its predecessors. Curvaceous lines with high-tech, bulletproof materials have replaced those bulbous forms made of translucent vinyl. The designs of inflatable boats are relatively simplistic, but there's more here than first meets the eye. Modern inflatables, with their sleek lines, gently sweeping upturned bows and sterns, and increased rigidity, are eminently practical and amazingly efficient pieces of outdoor gear.

Inflatable kayaks differ from one another in more than just size. They also vary in bow and stern lift, number of air chambers, size and shape of buoyancy tubes, placement of cross tubes, and location of air valves. How an inflatable handles on the river is largely dependent on its design, and many features contribute to a boat's safety as well.

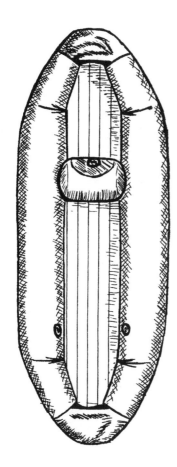

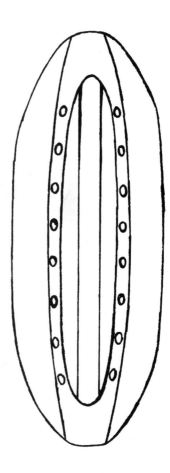

Top view   Bottom view

The inflatable kayak. The sophistication of design, materials, and manufacturing techniques has led to a whitewater boat to be reckoned with. Note the self-bailing floor.

An inflatable kayak is a very safe craft for a number of reasons. Its wide beam allows it great stability in whitewater. The boat is also very responsive, permitting quick maneuvers through rocky rivers. By its nature, the inflatable kayak is extremely buoyant. And lastly, the paddler of an inflatable kayak does not have to worry about entrapment because the boat has no deck like a hardshell kayak.

Materials determine the boat's weight and therefore its ease of handling. Boats with a slicker surface move more quickly across the water. Manufacturing techniques affect design by the number of seams used (fewer seams produce greater rigidity) and how tight the floor is (the tighter the floor, the faster the boat).

Size. Inflatable kayaks typically range in size from 9 to 10 1/2 feet for a one-person model, and from 11 to 12 1/2 feet for a two-person model. Larger and smaller models are also available.

The larger models have greater capacity for gear but are more difficult to maneuver because it takes longer to

The tandem boat. CECIL KUHNE

pivot once a stroke is made. A larger boat is more stable, however, which may be important on rivers with big waves. Smaller boats, which draw less water and are easier to maneuver through rocky stretches, may be necessary when the river is low, and they are more exciting, if that's what you're looking for.

Shape. Most inflatable kayaks have sharply pointed bows and sterns, formed by the buoyancy tubes as they taper toward the ends. One notable exception is the boat made by SOAR, which is blunt at both ends and is described by the manufacturer as an inflatable *canoe.*

Lift. An upturned bow and stern are important for two reasons: easier pivoting (a shorter waterline is created) and less water entering the boat (though a few boaters prefer low bows, where the boat drives through the rapids rather than rising over them). The boat's spin—its quick turning response to paddling strokes—largely depends on the curve of its bottom.

There are disadvantages to extreme lift. Capacity for storage of gear is reduced. Large waves have a greater effect, and wind blowing upstream can turn the bow into a sail, making downstream progress a real chore.

Tube Size. The size of the boat's tubes is important for the same two reasons—how the boat handles and the amount of water taken in while running rapids. Compared with other craft, the inflatable has low sides. But the low sides may cause the huge wave that capsizes a boat with higher sides to actually improve the equilibrium of a shallow one by filling it up (even if only momentarily, as in self-bailers). So, on the theory that it's more important to be balanced than dry, the IK's sides are low.

The main advantage of larger tubes is that less water will enter the boat. The added weight of water renders a boat sluggish and difficult to control, especially with conventional nonbailing floors. Larger tubes also provide more flotation—an important safety factor—and greater capacity for gear. Larger tubes affect handling, however, as they require more effort to move with a paddle.

Rigidity. Most boaters prefer a rigid design because it reduces drag and drives better through the rapids. Some boaters, however, prefer a more flexible design that allows the boat to break and fold as it encounters whitewater.

Self-bailing floors provide a more rigid boat; this is especially true of the foam floors, which provide stiffness similar to a hardshell boat. Rigidity also depends on materials and manufacturing techniques. Materials that stretch little under stress, such as polyester, generally produce boats more rigid than those made of nylon. Boats made with fewer seams are also more rigid because less bending of the boat is possible.

MATERIALS

The early IKs were made of unsupported vinyl, followed by various versions of reinforced vinyl. But most newer inflatable kayaks are made of coated fabrics. The base fiber provides strength and resistance to tearing, and the coating provides airtightness and resistance to abrasion.

The World War II assault rafts were made from cotton canvas. This was soon replaced by nylon, which is still common, although polyester is increasingly used. Neoprene, a synthetic rubber polymer, was the standard coating for many years, but this has been upgraded by the more durable, and expensive, Hypalon, a product of DuPont. A much cheaper version of neoprene, called EDPM, is used on economy boats, but it does not have nearly the resistance or longevity of neoprene or Hypalon. Newer "plastic" coatings—PVC (polyvinyl chloride) and urethane—have recently appeared, and their manufacturers claim they are even more durable than neoprene and Hypalon. All of these materials are made from a variety of polymers that can be mixed to provide infinite combinations with different characteristics.

BOAT MANUFACTURE

The manufacturing of inflatables is simple to describe but difficult to accomplish. Most inflatables are made by cutting panels from fabric and then seaming them together. The material is unrolled on a cutting table, a pattern is placed on top, and all the plies are cut at once by a rotary blade knife. The resulting pieces, marked to identify their location on the boat, are then spread out on worktables. Holes for air valves are cut and the valve cores attached to the material.

The sides of the boat are assembled first. The pieces of material that make up each side tube are seamed together. An additional piece of material can be attached to the bottom of the boat; this is sometimes called a chafing strip or wrapped floor. Most manufacturers use seams that overlap, though some use butt seams, which just touch each other and are held together with seam tape.

How seams are sealed depends on the material used and the manufacturer's preference. All materials can be sealed with a cold-cure adhesive that dries with time. Vulcanization, the original method of sealing, is used on a special uncured neoprene that is placed in a steam-pressure autoclave for curing. A third method, limited to PVC and urethane, involves heat or high-frequency radio waves, which provide a seal that is cured instantly. One manufacturer, Maravia, then sprays a urethane coating over the entire PVC boat.

Next the side tubes of the boat are attached at the ends. The boat's cross tubes (thwarts), if any, are then set into place. They may be glued on, clipped in, or laced into sleeves that are attached to the boat.

There the boat is, limp as a dishrag and ready to be inflated to low pressure for installation of the floor. The floor is attached to the bottom of the tubes, and V-tape is applied to the inside of the tubes where they meet the floor. The V-tape adds strength and will keep sand and pebbles from wearing away the main seam between floor and tube. With detachable self-bailing floors, the floor is

The introduction of Hypalon, PVC, and urethane coatings has made inflatables more durable than ever. COURTESY OF *MARK LISK/AIRE, INC.*

manufactured separately, but the grommet strip or piano hinge, for lacing in the self-bailing floor later, is attached in the same manner as a conventional floor. The boat is now complete except for accessories like D-ring patches and chafing strips.

A slight new variation on the traditional way of manufacturing inflatables is used by AIRE and employs a double skin: a rugged outer shell of PVC-coated polyester and then an inner shell of urethane-coated nylon, a thinner material. If a puncture tears both, you simply unzip the outer shell and replace the inner shell—just like a bicycle inner tube.

3

Buying an Inflatable Kayak

A number of years ago, selecting an inflatable kayak was easy. Paddlers were basically limited to the Tahiti, a thin vinyl "inflatable canoe" imported from France. They were cheap and fun to paddle—until, that is, you tried to run serious whitewater or carry a load in them. The fun ended when you tired of bailing or hit a sharp rock and punctured the tube.

Manufacturers of quality whitewater rafts are now making inflatable kayaks that are as tough and dependable as their line of rafts. Dozens of different models are now distributed across the country, with new manufacturers frequently coming onto the scene. Deciding which model to purchase has become more difficult as a result of the wide array of designs, features, materials, and coatings.

You must first decide how your boat will be used. What kinds of rivers will you typically paddle? A wider boat with large tubes is more appropriate for high-volume rivers and large rapids; a narrower, shorter boat is better suited to low-volume rivers with lots of rocks. If you'll be running rocky rivers, you'll need a model with a tough skin. If you want to play in rapids or surf your boat, a smaller model is more appropriate. If you're interested in

A quality boat can last a decade or more. COURTESY OF KERN RIVER TOURS.

using your boat for extended wilderness expeditions, make sure it has enough capacity to carry the load. For day trips on mild rivers, an inexpensive vinyl model may well suit your needs.

Costs of inflatable kayaks vary dramatically, depending on the materials used and the number of features. Inexpensive vinyl models can be had for $150 or so, but good-quality models made from the best materials can cost $1,000 or more. Cost of labor is a major factor here. Low-priced vinyl IKs have robotic-welded seams, whereas costlier models are built more by hand. The materials used in construction also greatly affect costs. A light vinyl is much less expensive than a heavy-duty coated fabric. Self-bailing floors also add significantly to a boat's price. Remember, though, that a quality boat, maintained properly, can last a decade or more.

MATERIALS

Consider, first, the strength of the base fabric. Fabrics used for inflatable boats are commonly rated by denier, a term of measurement that indicates a material's thickness and the weight of the threads used in weaving a fabric. Generally, the larger the denier number, the stronger and more durable the fabric, though this is not always the case. The floors of most good inflatables have a higher denier than the tubes because the floor takes more punishment. Extra layers of material on the floor are often offered by the manufacturer; these are called *wrap* floors.

The coating on top of the fabric is equally important. The coating protects the fabric and provides airtightness. It must also be resistant to the ultraviolet rays of the sun, which can break down a weak coating and cause an inflatable to develop leaks over time.

The finished coated fabric can be measured by several standards: weight, tear strength, and tensile strength. It's generally believed that the greater the weight, the stronger the material, but this may not always be so. Tear strength determines the number of pounds it takes to rip a piece of the fabric. Tensile strength, or breaking strength, may be the most useful measurement of all, as it determines the ability of the fabric to withstand tension.

Which coating to choose? The toughness, and price, of a Hypalon-coated material is generally based on the percentage of Hypalon used. A coating of 80 percent Hypalon, for example, is very durable, but it's also expensive. Various combinations of neoprene and Hypalon are available to reduce costs. PVC and urethane coatings may be equally strong and resistant to UV rays.

These new materials are expensive, and the paddler must decide whether the higher costs are worth it. As in most products, there is a law of diminishing returns. Those who desire the most rigid boat available usually choose a boat with polyester and PVC or urethane. But if you're interested only in material strength, the choice among coated fabrics is greater. One common mistake is to buy a boat whose material is not strong enough for its intended use. But it may also be possible to overbuy. If you plan to use the boat only in moderate whitewater for a few weeks each year, it may not be worthwhile to buy a boat with the strongest materials and the most options.

PERFORMANCE

The materials used in an inflatable kayak affect how it will handle on the water. Before good materials came into widespread use, all inflatable boats were viewed as inferior to hardshell craft because of their lack of rigidity. The vinyl tubes just couldn't accommodate enough air pressure to make a rigid boat, and over time the material would stretch out of shape, further decreasing the boat's firmness. Eventually, the boat's floors sagged, which increased drag and decreased maneuverability.

Lack of rigidity meant that the first IKs were always a little mushy, fine for bouncing off rocks but difficult to maneuver. They were also vulnerable to a phenomenon known as "tacoing," the unfortunate condition in which the craft folds in the middle so that bow and stern meet, much like a taco shell. Because of poor design and cheap materials, early IKs gained a bad reputation for being hard to control. But as tougher fabrics and coatings were developed, that reputation changed.

Rigid boats not only are more attractive, but they're safer and more maneuverable as well. Stiffer models also cut the wind better and shed more spray. The slick surface of a PVC or urethane coating allows the boat to slip more easily over the water's surface, giving these craft an edge on quickness and maneuverability.

PVC- and urethane-coated materials typically produce a more rigid boat than do Hypalon or neoprene. They are usually used on a polyester fabric, said to be stiffer than nylon, though some manufacturers do use a nylon fabric (said to be more durable than polyester) to produce a very stiff boat.

Other factors influence the IK's rigidity and performance. Solid floors of hard foam, tight inflatable floors, broad bottoms, and well-placed cross tubes or seats all help to maintain rigidity and thus stability. Keeping the air chambers inflated as tightly as possible also improves performance.

SIZE

Size is important because it determines not only capacity, but also how the boat handles. Smaller, narrower boats turn more quickly than larger, wider ones, but the bigger, broader designs are more stable and less likely to overturn in big water. Longer boats track better—that is, they hold a straight-line course without constant paddle correction—and they are superior in windy conditions. Consider too how compact an IK will be when rolled up, especially if you plan to take your boat on an airplane or stuff it into the trunk of your car.

Standard models are usually available in two sizes. The smaller ones are about 10 feet long and are sometimes classified as a one-person or K-1. Longer versions—up to 12 feet or so—are typically designated two-person or K-2 boats. A K-1 usually averages about 36 inches wide, and a K-2 will run up to 40 inches across. Tube sizes generally range from 10 to 13 inches.

The designation two-person is often a misnomer, because most IKs just aren't big enough to accommodate two people comfortably for any length of time. Coordinated paddling between two people is also difficult. Generally, two people who want to paddle together are better off using two separate IKs instead of a single large boat. A K-2 makes a great solo wilderness expedition boat because of the space available for carrying extra gear. Large or long-legged boaters may also be more comfortable in a two-person IK.

Also on the scene are play boats, nimble little IKs shorter than 9 feet. If you're interested in surfing waves, riding holes, or playing in eddies, the play boat is for you. There is no single design, but there are certain features that enhance a boat's ability to "play." The craft must be

K-2 travel requires packing lightly and coordinating paddling strokes between partners. COURTESY OF ADVENTURE BOUND, INC.

very rigid. A PVC or urethane coating produces a stiffer boat and also lessens the boat's drag. The polyester fabric used in most PVC- and urethane-coated craft also adds rigidity. Also important is a foam floor, which is stiffer than most inflatable floors.

Tube diameter also influences performance. It is generally proportional to boat length—the longer the boat, the larger the tube diameter—but some smaller models are designed with unusually large tubes. Generally, a K-1 will have tubes from 10 to 11 inches in diameter and a K-2 from 12 to 13 inches. Large tubes generate extra flotation so that an IK won't be swamped as easily in crashing waves. It's harder to fall out of an IK with big tubes, and they also increase carrying capacity. A model with large tubes may be perfect if you plan to paddle large, fast rapids.

Weight capacities are sometimes listed for boats. Exercise caution with this specification, because weight limits for inflatables are usually exaggerated. Overloading any whitewater boat is dangerous because it compromises maneuverability.

OTHER SPECIFICATIONS

Most modern inflatable kayaks are lightweight, between 15 and 40 pounds, with most models averaging 30 to 35 pounds. This is especially important when the IK will be packed into a remote area, via backpack, pack animal, or bush plane, or carried as baggage on commercial airlines. A lighter model may also prove beneficial when the boat must be portaged around rapids.

Also consider the boat's *rise*, or *kick*—how much the bow and stern curve up from the water. The amount of uplift influences maneuverability in several ways. A shorter waterline decreases the amount of friction between kayak and water and allows the boat to climb over the waves. On the other hand, it reduces the boat's stability and makes the boat more susceptible to wind. Bow rise used to be one of the most important design features because it reduced the amount of water entering the boat. With the advent of self-bailing boats, however, this feature has become less of a concern.

Most inflatable kayaks have a small spray shield of some kind. This feature was once considered essential to reduce the amount of water coming in over the ends. But with the advent of self-bailers, the spray shield also has become less important. Smaller shields still remain a basic part of many IK designs because they strengthen the area where the tubes come together, helping the tubes stay in position during impact with waves.

Valve design is also an important consideration. Valve failure while on the water can be dangerous. Avoid cheap valves, as well as those closed by detached plugs, which render an entire air chamber useless if the stopper is lost. Inexpensive screw-in valves need to be handled carefully to avoid leakage caused by cross threading. Military-style valves are strong and dependable. They operate on the simple principle of the right-hand thread: Screw counterclockwise to open, clockwise to close. Another popular design allows the valve to work one-way, automatically closing when the air pump hose is removed. (With the standard valve, air tends to leak out the valve during pumping.)

Placement of valves also deserves consideration. Watch for valves that might chafe when you're seated in the boat. Also beware of valves that are in hard-to-reach places, which will be especially difficult to access when the boat is loaded with gear.

MANUFACTURING TECHNIQUES

Before buying a kayak, carefully examine its seams. The lap seam method usually provides greater strength and boat rigidity, though butt seams may be fine if a wide seam tape is used. For either method, the seam tape should be at least an inch wide, preferably wider. Check the edges of the seam tape, making sure it has adhered to the boat without any gaps. Air bubbles in the seam tape indicate areas of poor adhesion.

For additional information on assembly techniques, ask the manufacturer. Most companies will provide details concerning the manufacturing process, since the methods are not always apparent from a visual inspection of the boat. For example, one manufacturing method orients the fabric's fill thread around the circumference of the tube rather than along the horizontal line of the kayak; this is said to provide greater rigidity and might be an important feature to consider.

The selling price of a kayak is only a rough indicator of the workmanship and materials employed in its manufacture. Ask other boaters and commercial outfitters about their experience with particular models. It is also important to learn which are the reputable and well-established manufacturers that will stand behind their warranties.

SEATS AND THWARTS

Seats for inflatable kayaks may take the form of inflatable cross tubes (called thwarts), rigid foam seats, or inflatable seats. They provide comfort and back support for the paddler and may also be an integral part of an IK's design by adding rigidity. Without some kind of substantial cross tube or seat, the boat's side tubes may bend inward under the crush of heavy waves.

The inflatable cross tube offers solid support for the paddler, though it usually isn't as comfortable as the other two styles for long periods of time. These tubes can be either integral or movable. Integral cross tubes can be a problem with two-person models, especially if the kayak will be used by just one person.

Rigid foam seats are usually more comfortable and versatile. They don't have to be inflated, and they are very durable. A foam seat will make the IK package a little bulkier, however, because the foam doesn't fold easily.

Inflatable seats are perhaps the most comfortable of all, and they can be custom inflated to suit each paddler's specifications. They add little rigidity to the IK, however, and are more prone to punctures.

Whatever seat you choose, be sure to secure it to the boat, especially in whitewater, to avoid losing it.

SELF-BAILING FLOORS

Most new inflatable kayaks are equipped with self-bailing floors, which offer tremendous advantages, especially in whitewater. Self-bailers are safer simply because water drains more quickly from them. But self-bailing boats vary considerably in their ability to drain quickly. The best ones bail themselves in a matter of seconds.

Self-bailing floors operate on two principles: holes in the bottom of the boat to allow water to drain back into the river, and elevation of the floor above the waterline to keep water from leaking into the boat through the drain holes.

There are two methods of elevating the floor. Rigid ethafoam may be inserted into the bottom of the IK over a traditional floor. In many models, a large hole is cut into each corner of the floor. The other method uses an inflatable floor in either furrowed I-beam or flat drop-stitch construction. The inflatable floor is usually laced into a grommet strip (or piano hinge) along the bottom of the boat. Occasionally, integral (or glued-in) inflatable floors, with drain holes like the rigid foam floors, are offered. To withstand abuse, inflatable floors must be constructed of very rugged materials. Inflatable floors may be flat or ridged with individual chambers. There's some disagreement over which is better. Those preferring flat floors claim they glide easier and aren't as affected by side currents. Those favoring ridged floors maintain that the corrugations "bite" the surface of the water and track better.

An IK with a foam floor won't fold into a small bundle, but one with an inflatable floor will. Despite the packing limitations, many paddlers prefer rigid foam floors because they improve performance. This is because the foam floor lies flatter on the water's surface than an inflatable floor and therefore offers less resistance. Foam floors require practically no maintenance and never lose air unexpectedly. But because of their stiffness, foam floors tend to be less comfortable for the paddler.

Manufacturers greatly benefited from the self-bailing feature, as orders flooded in from kayakers replacing their old boats. But are they worth it?

Removing water from an inflatable kayak is a tedious chore. A self-bailing boat not only eliminates that drudgery, but improves safety as well. A boat that is full of water is heavy and difficult to maneuver, increasing the chances of the boat wrapping sideways on a rock or capsizing in large rapids, not to mention tearing a sagging floor.

The self-bailing option is expensive, however, and the additional material can add weight and bulk to a kayak. Some boaters also claim that the additional flotation of the floor causes the boat to ride higher on the water, thus increasing its tendency to flip in rapids. Most boaters would dispute this, however. Other detractors of the self-bailing floor maintain that the added stiffness of the boat increases its tendency to surf, and even slide backward, in waves. But again, most boaters would not agree.

Some boaters actually prefer water in their boats, because they believe the weight helps flush them through rapids. This may be true, as long as no quick maneuvering is necessary. But many rock-studded, high-gradient rivers never would have been successfully run without self-bailers.

A catamaran kayak. COURTESY OF LEON WERDINGER/JACK'S PLASTIC WELDING.

CATAMARAN KAYAKS

The idea of using a couple of inflatable tubes with a frame holding them together began when Colorado River outfitters used huge surplus pontoons to ply the waters of the Grand Canyon. Several outfitters in California then started using shorter tubes in the 13- to 15-foot range for their smaller volume rivers. Now there are even smaller catamaran kayaks on the market, such as the one-person "catyaks" from Jack's Plastic Welding.

The advantage of catamarans is obvious at first glance: There is no need for bailing. The open center seems awkward, however, when you're used to a floor beneath your feet, so many boaters install a floor of some kind, which allows for better footing and storage of gear.

Catamaran advocates claim they are ideal for rocky rivers, since the chance of hitting rocks is reduced by half. When broached against a rock or canyon wall, the catamaran allows water to pour through its center rather than filling up and becoming lodged in place. These boats are also extremely stable because of the "bite" the two pontoons have on the water.

Catamaran kayaks also have a place in expedition boating, as they pack into smaller pieces than the typical kayak. But the frame for a catamaran is by necessity more complicated, though a number of catyaks are now frameless, with the tubes held together by an inflatable floor.

A catamaran, however, cannot be as heavily laden as a conventional inflatable, since it doesn't have the flotation of a floor. Many boaters claim that catamarans are more sluggish because the current doesn't have as much purchase on the boat. Catamarans may also be slightly more difficult to maneuver when the boat moves sideways, because the current has a greater influence on the downstream tube, against which it is pushing and accumulating.

4

CUSTOMIZATION, MAINTENANCE, AND REPAIR

Few pleasures can match that of messing around with boats, and the inflatable kayak is no exception. If the boat doesn't arrive from the factory just as you like it, you can have it customized. Make certain, however, that any modifications you make will not hamper your ability to escape from the boat if it overturns.

River running can be pretty tough on inflatables. But a good-quality boat will last for many years if careful maintenance is done on a regular basis. And maintenance will not only lengthen the life of your boat, but will also reduce the number of repairs needed on loose seams and patches.

CUSTOMIZING AN IK
To increase the safety and comfort of your boat, you may wish to add several features. If your boat doesn't have D-rings in the right places, you can buy additional D-ring patches and glue them where you need them. D-rings are essential for strapping down gear, especially for wilderness expeditions. And they make useful points for securing bow and stern lines. All in all, you can hardly have too many D-rings.

Thigh straps and foot braces hold the body in place with no risk of entrapment if the boat overturns.

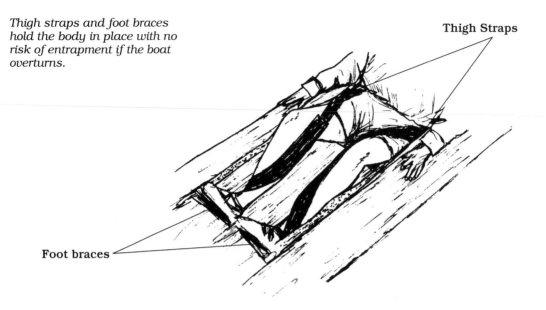

Thigh Straps

Foot braces

For additional stability, paddlers tackling big whitewater often add thigh braces, usually made from ethafoam and glued to the sides of the boat. The principle of thigh braces is simple: You tuck your thighs underneath them, and flex your muscles or bend your legs to hold yourself in place. You can easily exit the boat if it overturns by relaxing your legs. Braces from webbing material are also available. These are more adjustable than foam braces, and if you don't want to use them, you can tuck them out of the way.

Some paddlers carve footholds into ethafoam floors or install foot braces (in the form of ethafoam blocks or adjustable sliding braces found in rigid kayaks) in the bows of their boats. These are used to increase the likelihood of staying in the boat without risking entrapment should it flip.

A simple line or strap attached around the middle of the IK can serve as a flip line, giving you a secure handhold should the IK flip, as well as an easy way to overturn the boat. The strap should be attached in such a way that it won't slide out of place or entangle you.

Finally, to extend the life of IKs made of less-durable materials, some boaters add their own wrap floor—a second layer of fabric glued over the floor and lower side tubes. (For further information on how to add wrap floors, see "Repair Techniques" on pages 29–32.)

CONVERTING YOUR BOAT INTO A SELF-BAILER

An inflatable kayak with a standard floor can be converted into a self-bailer. First, cut four drain holes into the floor. Using a razor-blade tool, many boaters cut two 2-by-6-inch holes at each end of the boat where the IK's upturn begins. Glue boat fabric around these drain holes to strengthen them (for information on glues and the application of boat material, see "Repair Techniques" on pages 29–32). Then cut a sheet of thick closed-cell foam to closely conform to the interior of your boat. The thickness of the foam needed will depend on both the boat and your weight. Generally, 4 to 6 inches is best. The edges of the foam should allow full drainage. Cut openings in the foam sheet to match the drain holes in the floor.

Elevating the floor *above* water level is the key. A removable air mattress is standard in some IKs and can often be combined with 2 inches of foam above it to make a self-bailer. (The air mattress alone won't make a good self-bailer because incoming water gets trapped between the mattress and the floor material, causing the floor to sag.) Be sure and cut the foam to allow drainage; the inflatable floor, because it is smaller, does not need to be cut.

MAINTENANCE

Some maintenance is preventive. Wear on a boat often occurs while transporting it to and from the river. As the car or truck bounces, the boat rubs against a protruding object; this eventually abrades the coating in that spot. To prevent this type of wear, place the boat in a tarp and load it away from any such abrading objects. Rope or nylon webbing used to tie the boat in a bundle can also abrade the boat's coating; be sure to remove these straps before transporting it. When unloading gear at the put-in point, prevent punctures by taking care not to step on the uninflated boat or drag it on rocky ground.

When inflating the boat, add air until the boat is at its proper operating pressure, which varies slightly from model to model but is usually about 2½ pounds per square inch. Using an air pressure gauge is the most precise method, but many boaters simply add air until the tube is drum tight and then test the tube by feel. (When the fist bounces off the tube upon striking it, it's ready.)

Because the bursting strength of most well-made boats is two or three times their operating pressure, the pressure can be somewhat higher without danger. It's best not to subject the boat to extremes, however. In very hot weather, you should take the time at lunch or while you're ashore late in the afternoon to check, either manually or with a gauge, the boat's air pressure, since the increased temperature may cause the adhesive to soften and weaken its bonding strength. Periodically release air to prevent unnecessary strain on the boat's seams and valves.

Before boarding the boat, rinse the sand off your shoes; if you don't, they'll act like sandpaper pads and scrape the coating off the boat's fabric. When you tie the boat to shore, do so in such a way that it will not rub against rocks and boulders.

Before deflating the boat at the end of your trip, stand it on one side at the river's edge and wash it out by splashing buckets of water into it. Take special care to remove any rocks lodged between the buoyancy tubes and the floor; these could puncture the boat as you roll it up for transportation back home.

At home, give the boat a more thorough cleaning than was possible at the take-out. Use mild soap and water to remove dirt, since harsh detergents and petroleum products can disintegrate the boat's coating. If soap doesn't remove the stains, rub the stain lightly with a soft scrub brush or soap-filled scouring pad until it disappears. Commercial rubber preservatives may also be used (I especially recommend 303 Protectant), but be sure they do not contain silicone. Silicone is slippery, making it hard for a paddler to stay in the boat in whitewater, and the slippery surface also makes it difficult to apply adhesive in case of repair.

After a thorough cleaning, let the boat air out and dry thoroughly. The boat should be tightly inflated so that air can reach the space between the floor and the buoyancy tubes. If the boat is not absolutely dry before storage, the moisture can weaken its seams, especially those surrounding the floor. The seams may be weakened so much, in fact, that the floor will fall out of the boat. It's also important to get rid of any water that may have found its way inside a buoyancy tube. Before storing the boat, leave its valves open for a couple of days to allow air to circulate inside the tubes and remove any moisture that may have accumulated there.

The boat's valves should also need to be cleaned periodically. Dirt can work its way into the valves' interior, causing abrasion of valve parts and stickiness of movement. To reduce this wear, clean the valves with a toothbrush soaked in soapy water. Occasionally lubricate the valves with a penetrating lubricant such as WD-40, but not with an oil that will attract dust and dirt.

Now the boat is ready for storage. If space allows it, it's best to store the boat fully inflated, because rolling or folding it tightly for an extended period creates a great deal of stress on its fabric, especially with PVC coatings. (Tightly rolling or folding a boat for short periods to transport it will not harm it, however.) If space prohibits storing the boat fully inflated, at least partially inflate it before rolling it up *loosely*. Store the boat in a cool, dry place, away from rodents, which love to chew on such materials.

REPAIR TECHNIQUES

Fabric ripping and air escaping are the worst sounds an inflatable boat owner can hear. Fortunately, with today's tough-skinned coated fabrics, such tears are relatively rare. But if a tear does occur, it need not, in most cases, present serious consequences. The other chamber (and the floor, if it's a self-bailer) will provide sufficient buoyancy to get the boat to shore for repair. Once ashore, temporary repairs sufficient for a quick return to the river can be completed. More permanent repairs can be made upon returning home.

Your basic repair kit, subject to minor alterations for the particular trip (more of the same materials for longer or extremely remote trips), should include the following items:

- Patching material (at least 1 square yard for extended trips or extremely rocky rivers where the likelihood of a large tear is great)
- Scissors
- Solvent
    For neoprene: toluene or methyl ethyl ketone (MEK)
    For Hypalon: toluene
    For PVC: MEK
    For urethane: toluene or MEK
- Adhesive (follow the manufacturer's recommendations)
- Roller

Repair of inflatables is not difficult, as long as a few basic guidelines are followed. Patching is the most common method of repair. The basic steps are as follows:

1. Cut the patch to fit.
2. If neoprene or Hypalon, scuff the patch and area to be patched.
3. Clean the area with a suitable solvent.
4. Apply two coats of adhesive to the patching surfaces.
5. Roll down the patch securely to the boat.

It is first necessary to find the leak. It can be difficult to determine the exact location of small tears and pinpoint holes in the boat. The best method of detecting these is to wipe soapy water over the surface of the tightly inflated boat. Any leaks in the boat's buoyancy tubes will cause air bubbles to appear. Repeat this procedure after the patch has been applied to ensure that the repair is airtight.

Before applying the patch to the boat, it may be necessary to completely deflate the entire section where the repair is to be made. This will give easier access to the area and allow the patch to be pressed down securely.

Small tears, not larger than an inch or two, may be repaired by a simple patch placed on the outside of the tear. On longer tears, for the most secure patch possible, it is advisable to fasten a patch inside the boat before applying one outside. If the boat is needed for immediate service and there isn't enough time to apply an inside patch, an outside patch alone is usually sufficient for the duration of the trip.

After you have located the tear, cut a patch from a sheet of coated fabric, preferably the same in weight and coating as the boat's material. In any case, the repair material must not be lighter in weight or the patch will swell in the middle. On smaller tears (2 inches or less) the patch should overlap the tear at least 1 inch in every direction. Larger tears will require more overlap to prevent the patch from blistering. Round off the edges of the patch, since square corners are easily pried up.

With neoprene- or Hypalon-coated boats, it is extremely important to scuff or abrade the area around the tear, as well as the bottom of the patch, to provide a secure interlock between the two surfaces. (PVC- and urethane-coated surfaces, however, should *never* be scuffed prior to patching.) Use a file, sandpaper, or steel wool to scuff the area until it is no longer glossy. If none of these are available, use a piece of sandstone or other abrasive rock. If the boat has been painted with a coating, it is essential to completely remove this top layer of coating from the area to be patched. Be especially careful, however, not to scuff the coating so deep that you expose the underlying fabric.

With any type of coating, it is necessary to clean the surfaces with a suitable solvent before applying glue. The solvent also serves to slightly soften the fabric's coating and thin the adhesive, so that they will bond better. Solvents should be used *sparingly*; if used in excessive quantities, the solvent can destroy the existing coating. In the case of neoprene or urethane coatings, the area should be scrubbed with a clean cloth soaked in toluene or methyl ethyl ketone (MEK). Hypalon surfaces should receive a thorough cleaning with a clean cotton cloth soaked in toluene. Vinyl surfaces, such as PVC, should be scrubbed with MEK and a scouring cloth until clean and no longer glossy, followed by a damp wipe with a clean cotton cloth soaked with MEK. Any solvent should be applied with care because of its strong fumes and high flammability.

For a secure bond, be sure to use the correct adhesive for your particular fabric coating. Check with the manufacturer for the best brand. If possible, avoid extremes in air temperature when applying the adhesive. For most adhesives, 70 to 85 degrees F. is optimum. For an emergency repair, however, conditions for patching may be modified, to some extent, to account for deviations in temperature. In warmer temperatures, you may have to apply more adhesive, since it dries faster, or provide shade over the area to be glued. More difficult problems occur when the temperature is cold, since the adhesive may not completely dry. About the only alternative in cold weather is to heat the surfaces to be patched with a small fire, camping stove, or heated Dutch oven lid placed nearby before you apply the adhesive. Be careful, though, not to place an open flame near the adhesive, which is very flammable.

Apply adhesive evenly to both the area surrounding the tear and the patch itself. A thin layer is usually sufficient. Allow the first layer of adhesive to dry completely, then apply a second coat.

The curing time before applying the patch varies according to the adhesive used. Follow the manufacturer's instructions. In any case, the adhesive should be allowed to dry slightly beyond the tacky stage before applying the patch. Place your finger on the adhesive; it should *not* stick. If it does, the adhesive needs to cure longer.

After you have put the patch in place, press it down with a roller or other hard object. Start rolling or pressing from the middle of the patch, and move toward the edges. This will remove any air bubbles trapped under the patch. Then press down the edges securely. After firmly pressing down the patch, spread additional adhesive around its edges to secure it further.

If possible, allow the adhesive to cure overnight before reinflating the damaged chamber. If not, at least allow the repair to dry for several hours, and keep the tube loosely inflated until the next morning. The patch will probably suffice for the remainder of the trip, but the tear should probably be repatched later and perhaps an inside patch added for a stronger repair. To remove an old patch for later repairs, direct the heat of a 1000-watt (or more) hair dryer over the area, and as the adhesive loosens, pull the patch off with a pair of pliers.

5

Accessories

You've selected a boat. Now you need a number of accessories to get you going: a paddle, an air pump, a life jacket, the proper clothing, a helmet if you're running whitewater, a rescue rope, waterproof containers, and so on.

PADDLES

The double-bladed kayak paddle is favored for the inflatable kayak because it eliminates the need for switching hands. Single-bladed canoe paddles are inadequate for IKs, because you need to stroke on both sides of the IK for maximum efficiency, as inflatables lack the keel that makes a hardshell boat track well. And paddlers in IKs sit too low for effective stroking with a single-bladed paddle.

The paddler has a choice of two types of paddles: feathered and nonfeathered. Some breakdown paddles offer both options. The blades of a feathered paddle are set at right angles to each other; on a nonfeathered paddle, they're parallel. When using a feathered paddle, the blades must be rotated so that when one blade is moving through the water, the other blade presents just its edge to the wind. This decreased wind resistance makes for easier paddling. The stroke also takes advantage of the

The kayak paddle's various styles.

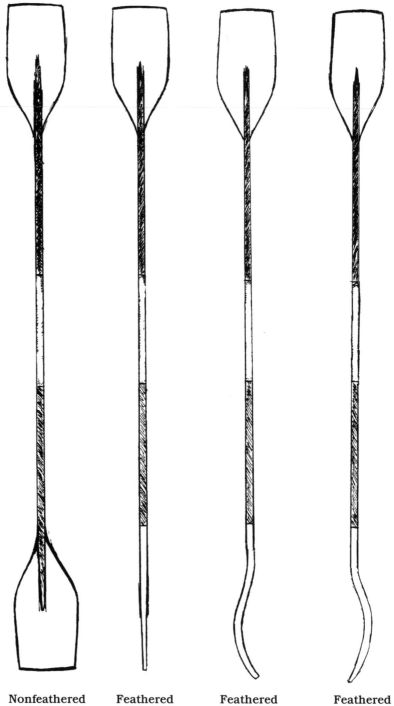

Nonfeathered   Feathered with flat blade   Feathered with spoon blade (right-hand control)   Feathered with spoon blade (left-hand control)

natural roll of the wrists and is therefore more efficient. Some paddlers begin with a nonfeathered paddle and then switch to a feathered paddle as their proficiency increases.

How a paddle performs is largely the result of its material. Wood is traditional. Boaters like the way it flexes with the stroke, a feel many say cannot be duplicated with a synthetic. Wood doesn't readily assume the temperature of water or air, so it's more comfortable, and the lamination process can produce a paddle with great strength and light weight. But quality varies greatly among manufacturers and models, so beware.

Other paddles have plastic or fiberglass blades, which are durable, lightweight, and require almost no maintenance. Their shafts are typically fiberglass or aluminum. Fiberglass shafts not only are strong and light, but also offer good flexibility; aluminum shafts are sturdy and inexpensive but are stiff and therefore more tiring to use.

The length of the paddle you should use depends on the size of the boat's tubes, your height, your position in the boat, and your personal preference. Perhaps the most important factor is your height sitting down. The paddle should not be so short that you must lean out of the boat to make a stroke, nor so long that the stroke is made with the arms above the head. Kayak paddles are typically $7^1/_2$ or 8 feet in length, though they are sometimes a foot shorter for smaller people or for those without much upper-body strength. An excessively long paddle makes for an inefficient stroke, so it's best to err on the short side.

Wide blades deliver more power and are suitable for all conditions except strong headwinds, when the blades may slow you down. Beginners should stick with flat-bladed paddles rather than spoon paddles, which are curved on one side of the blade. With a spoon-bladed paddle, the curved surface must always be in the proper position to be effective; in whitewater, an inexperienced paddler can easily get the blade surfaces confused. For experienced paddlers, these paddles minimize splashes and increase the efficiency of each stroke by biting into the water better. A spooned blade's *power face* is the side that addresses the water, the inside of the spoon.

Breakdown paddles, which can be taken apart, are typically made of aluminum and covered with plastic. In addition to offering easy storage and transport, the paddle's breakdown design allows you the option of feathering the blades, and if you feather those with spoon blades, to change from left- to right-hand control.

A paddle should be comfortable to hold. Look for a smooth shaft that won't blister your hands. Several methods exist for protecting palms from the stress of the rotating shaft. The simplest is to wear gloves, some of which are made specifically for whitewater use.

Drip guards, little plastic rings that keep water from dribbling down the shaft toward your hands, are nice to have but not essential.

Your paddle is your boat's sole means of propulsion, so treat it kindly. Don't push off rocks with your paddle blade or use it as a lever to pry the boat free.

Paddle repair in the field is difficult. Duct tape wrapped around the shaft may hold it together if necessary. In case of joint failure, find a sturdy stick, position it over the broken joint, then secure with duct tape. Bent paddle shafts or blades can often be straightened by simply applying your weight against them.

AIR PUMPS

Air transforms the limp and lifeless form of an uninflated boat into a firm and sturdy craft capable of running the toughest whitewater successfully. Sufficient pressure enables the boat's design features to function most effectively, since a boat is more rigid when it is properly inflated. Rigidity not only provides greater maneuverability, but also helps the boat drive through rapids without a "porpoising" motion. This rigidity also helps to prevent a boat, when broaching against a rock, from wrapping around it.

Since all boats lose a little air during the day, and because air contracts during the cool morning air, most boats require a little inflation each morning before another day's run. Most boaters prefer to run large rapids with a rigid boat because it offers greater control, so more air may be added at that time. And if the boat is suddenly punctured, an air pump is necessary to reinflate the chamber after repair. Air pumps used for inflatable kayaks differ from the typical tire pump, since IKs require a large volume of air at low pressure rather than a small volume of air at high pressure.

Types of Air Pumps. Air pumps vary both in method of inflation (electric or manual) and in amount of capacity (and thus the time necessary to inflate a boat). Different pumps may be used for different purposes. One may serve for the initial inflation at the put-in, while another is packed away for topping off the boat on the river. Air pumps with the capacity to deflate a boat are also useful, since removing all the air from a boat for its transport back home can be a difficult task.

When an electric power source is available, an electric air pump is the easiest method of inflating the boat. Some models operate on household electric current, and others can be plugged into a car's cigarette lighter or clipped to its battery.

Another method of initial inflation is a large cylinder pump, usually about 2 feet high and 4 to 6 inches in diameter. These pumps are operated like a standard bicycle pump and have two foot pedals for stability while pumping. Many large cylinder pumps also allow deflation of the boat by switching the hose from the bottom to the top of the pump. Foot-operated bellows pumps are easier to operate than small hand pumps, especially when pumping becomes more difficult as a result of increased air pressure inside.

Both large-volume cylinder pumps and foot bellows pumps require stability for their operation and are therefore easier to use if placed on the ground. To top off the boat while in it, the best pumps are those operated by hand—either a bellows pump with handles or a small-volume cylinder pump (about 12 inches long and 3 inches in diameter), both of which are compact and eas-

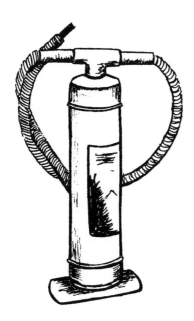

Cylinder and bellows air pumps.

ily carried on the boat. A pump is a necessity for survival on the river; lash it securely to the boat to prevent its loss in whitewater.

Many air pumps, especially the high-quality electric models and the large cylinder pumps, are fairly expensive, so you should examine the features carefully before purchasing one.

- Check that the pump contains the correct fittings to either screw or fit closely into the valve of your boat. A secure fit is especially important for pumps used to top off the boat.
- Check the total volume of the pump, measured in either cubic inches or cubic feet. This volume determines the speed of inflation. A larger volume allows quicker inflation.
- Check whether the pump is reversible, thus allowing deflation as well as inflation.
- With hand and foot pumps, the action should be easy and smooth, requiring as little effort as possible.
- With cylinder pumps, those with fewer parts are preferable, for two reasons: The possibility of malfunction is reduced, and the disassembly of the pump is simplified (especially important for repairs in the field).
- Check whether the pump can be taken apart with only a screwdriver or pliers, or if special tools are required. It is also desirable that a cylinder pump have components that, for the most part, can be obtained at a local hardware store.
- Note the number of metal parts in a cylinder pump. It should contain a minimum number that will corrode if wet. Find out if the pump is immersible to determine whether water will damage its internal parts. Most metal fittings will corrode and rust if wet, and pumps that are not immersible will have to be kept in a waterproof container. Immersible pumps require less care and may even be used as bilge pumps if other bailing equipment is lost.
- With bellows pumps, look for strong springs and durable hinges. Here, quality is usually commensurate with price.

Care. Keep the pump in a container to protect it from collision, dirt, and water. Even an immersible cylinder pump may have a leather plunger, and constant wetting and drying of the plunger will eventually deteriorate it. Water inside bellows pumps is difficult to remove completely, and the internal spring may rust. If you have an electric pump, do not use it as a deflator unless it is designed for that purpose.

Lubricate cylinder or hand pumps regularly to provide ease of operation, deter rust, and prevent the seal of the plunger from drying out. These seals are ordinarily made of leather or rubber and are lubricated with water, oil, graphite, or petroleum jelly, depending on the particular model. Check with the manufacturer to determine the proper lubricant. The wrong lubricant can damage the seal of the pump's plunger. Lubrication will normally revive a dry seal, but eventually the seal may have to be replaced if completely worn or dried out.

Repair. Most well-made cylinder pumps are durable, and their simple design enables easy repair. If a fitting of a cylinder pump is worn or corroded, it will be necessary to disassemble the pump and replace the defective part. Many pumps are easy to take apart with just a screwdriver or pliers. Most pump parts are available at hardware stores, but some, especially die-cast parts, must be ordered from the pump manufacturer. Plunger seals, too, are usually available only from the manufacturer, so it's a good idea to have an extra on hand. The hose of cylinder pumps may develop splits after seasons of hard use. Small tears in the hose can be repaired with friction tape or silicone rubber sealant. If these repairs fail, replace the hose.

LIFE JACKETS

Few pieces of boating gear have progressed more in comfort and safety than the life jacket—great news for whitewater boaters.

Different types of life jackets, or personal flotation devices (PFDs), as the Coast Guard calls them, have been designed specifically for rafting or for kayaking. The kayaking PFDs, called Type III Buoyant Devices, while thinner and more comfortable to wear, offer less flotation than most rafting PFDs. The rafting PFDs, classified as Type V for specialized whitewater use, have become popular because of their additional flotation.

Other types of life jackets, unsuitable for kayaking, are the Type I, a bulky, orange jacket filled with kapok; Type II, a horse-collar-style jacket; and Type IV, a buoyant seat cushion.

Personal flotation device.

For safety when kayaking, you'll need a Type III or Type V PFD filled with closed-cell foam. The best life jackets are made with Ensolite foam, which is soft and conforms to the body's contours for comfort. Type III PFDs, usually shorter and having flotation "ribs" rather than "slabs," are designed for canoeists and kayakers and give more freedom of motion. Type V PFDs are specially designed for whitewater, generally with commercial raft passengers in mind. These jackets offer greater flotation and safety than the Type III but tend to be bulkier and more restrictive.

When choosing a life jacket, favor safety over comfort. Because of your sitting position in the inflatable kayak, some long-waisted life jackets may be unsuitable. PFDs designed for hardshell kayakers often have extra flotation in the area below the waist, which can be flipped up for comfort. The amount of flotation you require in a life jacket depends on your body's own flotation, your experience, and the kind of whitewater you'll be tackling. A beginner will be better off with a "high-float" jacket—one with at least 22 pounds of flotation—because they're safer. An experienced paddler familiar with swimming in rapids may not require as much flotation. For easy rivers, a "shortie" Type III offers a good measure of safety and the advantage of unrestricted motion. In big whitewater, a Type V or a high-flotation Type III is better.

The life jacket should have sufficient buckles and straps to secure it firmly about your body. The PFD must be worn snugly to keep it from riding up over your head, so make certain you buy one that fits well. Most Type IIIs are sold by chest size, while a Type V rafting PFD is one-size-fits-all and requires more adjustments. Fit is important to safety, especially for children and smaller adults.

Always fasten *all* buckles, zippers, and waist ties when you put the life jacket on; *never* wear the PFD loose or open in the front. And pull the side adjustment straps down *snug*. This is also important so that you will not become entangled if the boat overturns. When you take off your life jacket, always clip it down so that the wind doesn't blow it away.

If treated properly, a good PFD will give you years of protection. Don't use it as a seat cushion. After each trip, hang it up to maintain its shape and prevent mildew. Clean it often, following the manufacturer's recommendations, using a mild soap to avoid harming the internal foam.

CLOTHING

Veteran river runners agree when it comes to clothing: Buy the best and cut corners somewhere else. A boater's enjoyment is too dependent on climate and water temperature to do otherwise. With new synthetic fabrics and insulation—incorporated into clothing designed just for river runners—there's no reason to be uncomfortable.

The most versatile system involves layering, with clothing added or removed to regulate the body's heat: Layers are removed during periods of exertion and added during periods of rest, the usual routine on river trips. Start with an inner layer of long underwear, add additional layers of insulation as needed, and then top it off with a waterproof shell.

If there's the slightest chance you'll get wet (and there usually is), synthetic fabrics don't retain water and will dry quickly. Because of this characteristic, pile and fleece work well. The effectiveness of these materials depends largely on their thickness. They are extremely rugged and require little care. The only drawback is their bulk: They don't compress well for packing.

If the weather or water will be very cold, you'll need long underwear. Polypropylene is popular because it keeps moisture off the skin. Polyester fabrics (under trade names like Capilene) pill less and remain softer than polypropylene. Even though these materials don't offer much insulation, the body stays warmer when it's dry. Different thicknesses of these fabrics are available

Paddling jacket.

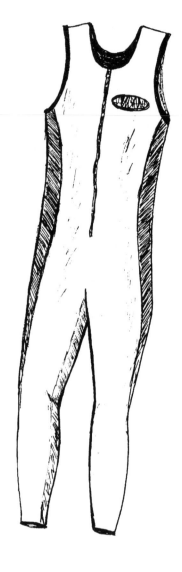

Wetsuit and booties.

for diverse situations. In even colder weather, you can add more layers of the thinner synthetic fabrics or use a thicker synthetic fill. For use on the river, goose or duck down is useless, because it takes days to dry. Wool is a good insulator when wet, though it becomes heavy, stretches, and is slow to dry. With the synthetics on the market, wool has lost most of its appeal.

A waterproof outer layer—raincoat and pants, paddling jacket, or drysuit—is necessary to keep the inner layers dry and prevent heat loss. Kayakers were the first to recognize the advantages of a waterproof shell when they developed the paddling jacket with its tight-fitting closures. Then they added paddling pants, complete with neoprene ankle cuffs or drysuit seals.

In frigid conditions, a neoprene wetsuit is commonly used, because the thin layer of water that is trapped underneath it is warmed by the body's heat. A drysuit—with a looser body and tight-fitting seals at neck, wrists, and ankles—allows insulation to be worn underneath. Many boaters find drysuits more comfortable, but they are more expensive and more difficult to maintain than wetsuits.

Don't forget the extremities—head, hands, and feet. The head is a critical area of heat loss—more than half of the body's heat can be lost through the head. Any type of hat will help, but a close-fitting wool or synthetic cap provides more warmth.

Drysuit.

Synthetic gloves work well to retain warmth when wet, but neoprene ones are even warmer, though they can be tiring to use because of the material's tendency to spring back to its original shape.

Wetsuit boots (with hard soles) and wetsuit socks (without) are the best protection against the cold water sloshing around in the boat. A thin, polypropylene liner sock underneath will keep your feet drier, and therefore even warmer. Wetsuit boots have become increasingly sophisticated, with zippers, lace-up tops, padded insoles, and traction soles. But if you will have to walk a long way, wetsuit socks with running shoes may be the most durable.

WATERPROOF CONTAINERS

A wide assortment of waterproof bags and boxes are available. Most boaters seem to prefer the soft surfaces of bags whenever possible, not just for the obvious impact reasons, but because a bag expands and contracts to fit its contents and the space it has to be squeezed into.

Waterproof boxes have their place, however—a camera box for example, as well as the kitchen box and toilet. A surplus ammunition box works well, and makes an

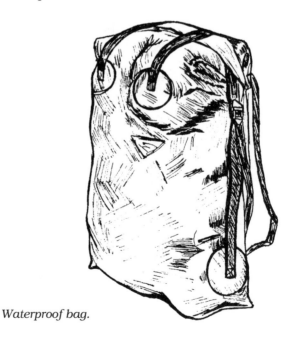

Waterproof bag.

excellent and totally waterproof camera box, but many boaters prefer plastic boxes because they're lighter and don't have the sharp edges that metal ones do.

OTHER GEAR

Helmets. These days IK paddlers, like hardshell kayakers, are beginning to wear helmets, mostly because they're challenging tougher, rockier rivers where helmets provide an important measure of safety. On easier waters, helmets aren't necessary, but when you start running more difficult whitewater, a helmet could save your life.

Helmet

The helmet you choose should be snug, but not so tight that it causes discomfort. The protective internal suspension is usually foam, but cheaper versions have plastic strapping. The helmet should have a chin strap to hold it in place. Whitewater helmets are designed with ear openings so that you can hear upcoming rapids and warnings from your fellow kayakers.

Lines. Ropes on the bow and stern are handy for securing the IK to shore. Many boaters consider 25 feet a good length for this purpose. Keep ropes safely stowed so that they don't become uncoiled and cause entanglement.

RIGGING

Rigging and tying down gear are important for both convenience and safety. When rigging a boat, pay attention to what you put where. Place personal items that will be needed during the day—cameras, sunglasses, suntan lotion, and a wind shell—in smaller containers that are easily accessible. The first-aid kit and air pump should also be handy, as well as your lunch.

Lash down the load securely. If tied down properly, gear won't be lost, even in a complete flip. Pack the equipment so that it's as low as possible. None of the baggage should protrude from the sides of the boat, and the gear should not interfere with paddling. The load should be balanced as evenly as possible on both sides of the boat.

Rather than tie everything down with ropes, many boaters prefer to use nylon webbing secured by heavy-duty buckles. It's faster and easier to use straps than to tie and untie knots.

6

PADDLING STROKES

It's a beautiful sight. Like birds' wings, paddles dip up and down, in and out of the water to steer the boat through rocky stretches of the river's rapids. Behind these graceful motions are inflatable kayakers working hard with the tools of the trade. Finesse, rather than brute strength, is ultimately the key to success in whitewater. The power of a river is simply too strong for it to be otherwise.

Two distinct skills are required: reading whitewater and executing the proper paddling strokes. When good technique is combined with knowledge of the river, a skilled boater can tackle the wildest of passages in this most graceful of endeavors.

Most anyone with average strength and coordination can become reasonably proficient in the basic paddle strokes after a few hours of practice. Beginning on flatwater is easier. For gaining confidence with the basic strokes, start on a lake or swimming pool. Then take your newly acquired paddling skills to a broad, slow river. You'll discover that handling the kayak is easier on moving water. The boat tracks better in a current, and because the flow gives you power, paddling is less work.

Practicing paddling skills.
CECIL KUHNE

On a swift stream without obstacles, the kayak moves along nicely, and a paddle stroke is needed only occasionally for keeping the course straight.

THE SITTING POSITION

Boarding the kayak is easy. Push the boat into the water. Holding the paddle in one hand and steadying the kayak with the other, lower yourself rear-end first into the middle of the boat. Then swing your legs into the bow. If your boat is equipped with thigh straps and footrests, position yourself into them. Grab your paddle, settle back against the seat or thwart, and you're off.

For greatest control of an inflatable kayak, sit slightly behind the center of the boat. Otherwise it won't respond as well to your strokes.

In self-bailing models, some water may enter the boat as you sit down; the amount will depend on your weight and the make of the boat. You may need to add an additional layer of closed-cell foam to the floor of the kayak to stay drier.

Boarding the kayak. CECIL KUHNE

A good sitting position gives you control of the boat. COURTESY OF MARK LISK/AIRE, INC.

HOLDING THE PADDLE

Paddling with feathered blades takes a little coordination, but soon the technique becomes second nature. Choose one hand to become the control hand, or *grip hand*. This is usually the right hand, even for left-handers. If the

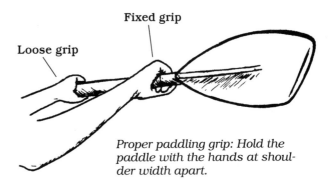

Loose grip   Fixed grip

Proper paddling grip: Hold the paddle with the hands at shoulder width apart.

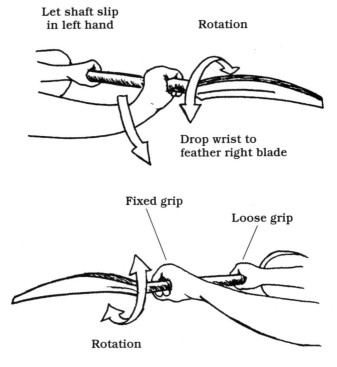

Let shaft slip in left hand   Rotation

Drop wrist to feather right blade

Fixed grip   Loose grip

Rotation

Feathering the paddle, using right-hand control (top), and left-hand control (bottom).

paddle has spoon blades, it will be designed for right-hand control; if it is a breakdown model, it can be so adjusted. The key to paddling with feathered blades is that the paddle *never* rotates in the grip hand. Firmly grip the paddle with the right hand, and let the paddle shaft rotate through your left. For left-hand control, do just the reverse.

When learning to paddle with feathered blades, some paddlers have trouble rotating the shaft so that the left blade is in the proper position, and the left blade slices through the water at the wrong angle. Watch the paddle blade as you stroke. Keep working on your technique until the maneuver becomes instinctive.

FORWARD STROKE

The forward stroke is the basic power stroke. It's made close to the side of the boat, with the paddle shaft moving on a vertical, or near-vertical, plane.

Begin the stroke by leaning forward, extending the lower arm full length, and bending the upper arm at the

The forward stroke. COURTESY OF B & A DISTRIBUTING.

elbow. Insert the blade into the water as far forward as comfortable, placing the blade close to the boat and dipping it almost completely into the water.

Pull directly backward with the lower arm while the upper arm drives forward at eye level. Pull backward with the lower arm until the hand is near the hip.

Then relax both arms, allowing the upper arm to drop down. This action causes the blade to rise to the surface of the water, and you can begin the stroke on the other side.

In executing the forward stroke, only a slight rotation of the body and shoulders should accompany the arm motion. Avoiding unnecessary body motion allows greater smoothness and efficiency.

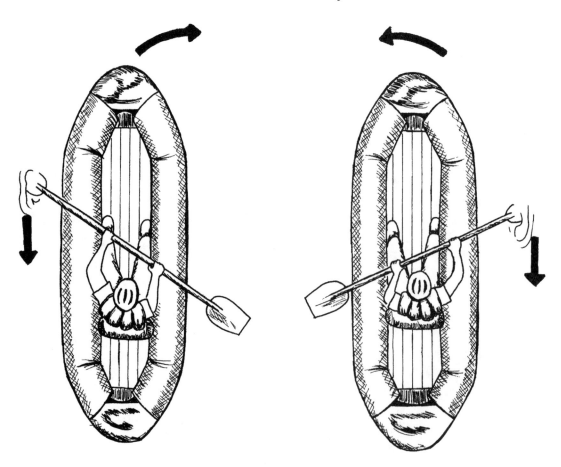

Forward power stroke. Paddle on the right side, the boat moves left; paddle on the left side, the boat moves right.

BACK STROKE

The back stroke is basically the reverse of the forward stroke. It begins where the forward stroke ends. The bottom arm pushes down and forward while the upper arm pulls up and back. Lean your body somewhat forward at the beginning of the stroke and somewhat backward at the end of the stroke. This stroke uses the muscles of the abdomen, arms, and shoulders, and it's necessary to keep a steady, erect posture.

In still water, the back stroke moves the boat upstream. In fast water, it slows the downstream speed of the boat, allowing for better visibility of obstacles downstream.

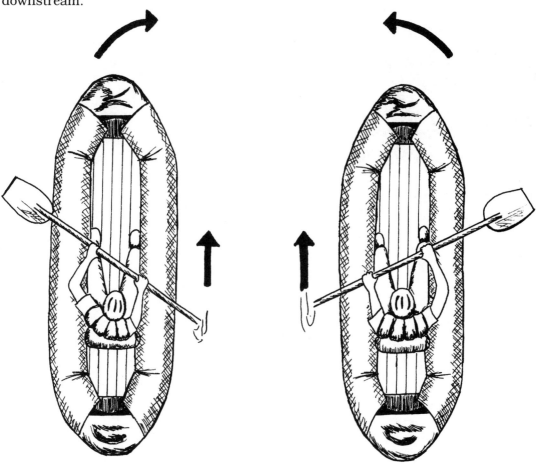

Reverse stroke. Paddle on the right side, the boat moves right; paddle on the left side, the boat moves left.

Practicing smooth strokes will lead to good form.
CECIL KUHNE

COMBINING THE STROKES

Don't worry too much about form at first; concentrate on making smooth, easy strokes. It's important to combine left-side and right-side paddling into one continuous smooth motion, with no hesitation in between. This delivers speed and power when you need it.

Balance is critical, too. Don't lean over the sides of the boat, straining too far for a stroke. Try to keep your back pressed against the seat, stroking with your arms, shoulders, and abdominal muscles, but *not* with your back.

TURNING

To make a right turn, you can either paddle forward on the left side or backpaddle on the right. To make a left turn, you do the opposite: paddle forward on the right side or backpaddle on the left. Backpaddling on the *same* side as the turn is easier for most beginners.

For faster turns with less effort, use your paddle blade as a rudder: While your boat is moving forward, submerge the blade, then, rather than pushing the blade away from you, just lean hard with your weight on the paddle in the backpaddle motion. A well-executed rudder stroke is handy when navigating rock-strewn rivers, where quick turns are necessary and there is little time or space to swing the paddle.

ADVANCED PADDLE STROKES

Once you've mastered the basic paddle strokes, you're ready to move on to advanced techniques.

The Sweep Stroke. For faster turning without losing forward momentum, use a forward sweep stroke; for quick pivoting, use a backward sweep. To execute a sweep stroke, you use the same basic stroking technique

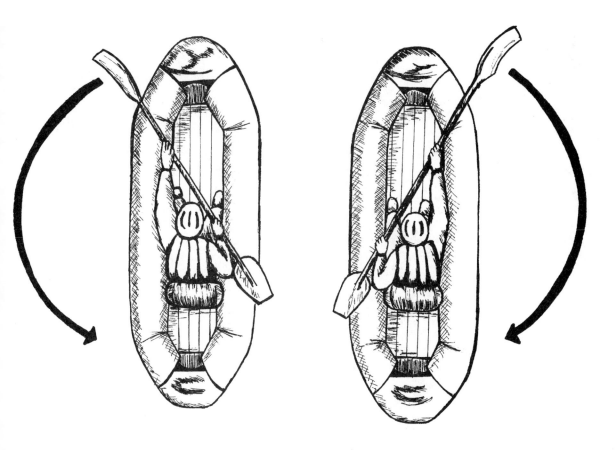

The arc of the sweep stroke adds power and speed to the basic forward and reverse strokes.

as for a regular forward or back stroke, except that you make an exaggerated reach with the paddle in a wide arc out and away from the boat. It's this extra reach that gives the stroke more power than a simple forward or back stroke.

The Brace Stroke. The *brace* stroke uses the paddle as a lever to provide stability. To execute the brace, hold the paddle straight out over the water, perpendicular to the middle of the boat. Then, with the blade face parallel to the water's surface, slap the blade down on the water's surface and lean hard onto the paddle.

A brace can be low or high. In the low brace, the power face of the blade is up and the elbows are above the paddle shaft. In the high brace, the power face of the blade is down and the elbows are below the paddle.

The low brace. COURTESY OF MARK LISK/AIRE, INC.

The low brace adds stability in rough water.

High brace. This stabilizing stroke can easily be converted to a propulsion stroke.

The high brace. COURTESY OF
MARK LISK/AIRE, INC.

The brace maintains balance, particularly in a high-side maneuver. With a brace, you're actually using the force of the river to keep the boat right side up. Always lean and brace *downstream*, not upstream, which would cause you to capsize.

The Draw Stroke. The draw stroke is used to quickly move the boat sideways. It resembles the movement of the brace stroke, except that it can be done on either the upstream or downstream side of the boat, and instead of leaning onto the paddle, you pull the blade toward the boat. To execute the draw stroke, hold the paddle blade straight out from the boat, submerge the blade, and pull it strongly toward you.

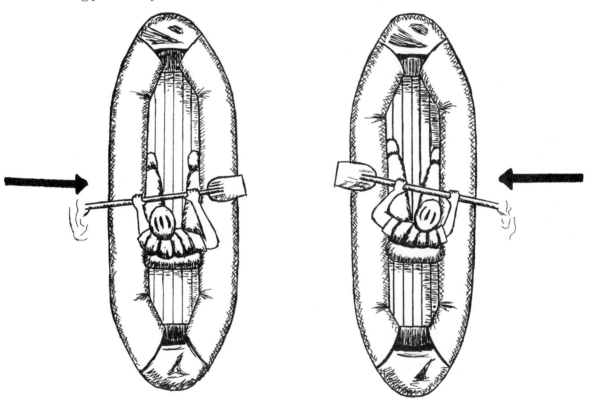

Draw stroke. This pull stroke moves the boat sideways quickly.

The Pry Stroke. The opposite of the draw stroke is
the *pry* stroke, a sideways push of the paddle away from
the kayak. Start the pry stroke with the paddle blade
near the side of the boat and with your upper arm over
the water. Push with your lower arm while pulling your
upper arm in toward you.

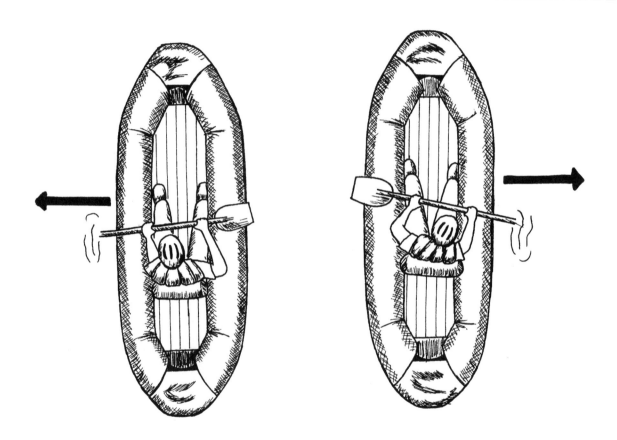

Pry stroke. This push stroke moves the boat sideways quickly.

7

RUNNING WHITEWATER

Reading whitewater is a special art that boaters have of evaluating a stretch of rapids to determine which route through the boulders and hydraulics will provide the least chance of damage to gear and to themselves. As with all fine arts, there is more than one way to do it well. With that said, there are still a few basic principles that allow boaters to better size up those intimidating rapids below.

Much can be learned about how a river works by simple observation. Spend time studying moving water and how it is affected by the obstacles it encounters. Observe rapids from downstream and notice where the rocks are located. Then walk up to the head of the rapids and look downstream to see how the rocks appear from a river runner's point of view. Watch other boaters run the rapids and observe where they position their craft.

Every river is different, yet all follow the same basic rules. Rivers basically vary according to volume, gradient, and velocity. A river with rapids that alternate with long quiet stretches, rather than dropping steadily over its length, is known as a *pool-and-drop* river. Such rivers are usually easier to run, simply because there is more time to recover below each stretch of rapids.

Reading whitewater. COURTESY
OF MARK LISK/AIRE, INC.

A river described as *technical*, on the other hand, has many tight, rocky passages that require finely tuned skills to negotiate. A river with a sizable volume of water and large rapids is known as *big water*. Boaters here can expect rapids with powerful waves, but big water tends to be straightforward, lacking the complicated obstacles that make maneuvering difficult.

RIVER HYDRAULICS

Running rapids requires an understanding of the river—its currents, form, and flow. Rapids are caused by a wide variety of factors, including the physical aspects of the riverbed and the volume of the river. The most obvious is the roughness of the riverbed, formed by rocks and boulders that have fallen from mountains and canyons or that have been swept into the main current by side streams.

Gradient. The steeper the gradient of the river as it flows downstream, the faster the water moves, normally rendering rapids more difficult to maneuver. Gradient is

This technical run challenges even the most experienced paddler. CECIL KUHNE

typically measured by the number of feet per mile the river drops. Usually, the greater the drop, the more dangerous the river.

But exceptions exist. Many dangerous rivers, notably the Colorado River through the Grand Canyon, have mild gradients, but long stretches of calm water drop suddenly into tremendous rapids. Other rivers have high gradients, but are easy to negotiate because the gradient is uniform or the riverbed smooth.

Constriction. Constriction of the river's current, caused by narrowing of the riverbanks or the presence of large boulders, also plays an important part in the river's difficulty. Constriction increases the river's velocity, sometimes dramatically.

Volume. The volume of the river has a definite effect on its whitewater. A large volume increases the river's speed and the force of its rapids, thus reducing the time you have to maneuver.

Generally, the greater the volume, the more difficult the rapids. This is not always the case, however. At low water, a rock may be clearly seen and avoided. At slightly higher levels, it may be possible to float over the rock, which merely creates a small wave. At even higher levels, there may be a reversal that must be avoided. At still higher levels, the reversal may be completely washed out.

River volume is measured in cubic feet per second (cfs), the amount of water passing a point every second. This measurement is relative; a smaller riverbed requires less volume for boating.

Add more water and you invariably increase the speed of the current. Changes in volume and velocity are important because water is heavy, weighing 8.33 pounds a gallon. A river flowing at a mere 1,000 cfs is backed by an incredible 62,400 pounds of force. A boat held broadside against a rock is therefore in a precarious situation. This is the same force, after all, that moves huge boulders around the river with little effort.

A river's volume can fluctuate greatly. Peak flows of snow-fed rivers typically occur during spring runoff. Their volume decreases through summer and early fall but increases quickly when it rains. When running unknown rivers, consult the proper sources about the current river volume and its suitability for boating.

A narrow, constricted part of a river is a chute.
COURTESY OF MARK LISK/AIRE, INC.

WHITEWATER RATINGS

In the whitewater community, both rivers and individual rapids are rated according to their degree of difficulty. The most common rating system, the International Scale of Whitewater Difficulty, uses a scale of Class I through VI, with Class I being easy water and Class VI virtually unrunnable. The ratings are subjective, however, and fluctuate considerably depending on the seasonal water level and whether there are drought or flood conditions.

The class ratings are as follows:

THE INTERNATIONAL SCALE OF WHITEWATER DIFFICULTY

Class I: Easy. Waves small; passages clear; obstacles easy to spot well in advance and avoid.

Class II: Novice. Rapids of moderate difficulty; passages mostly clear; some maneuvering required.

Class III: Intermediate. Waves numerous, high, and irregular. Rocks and eddies present. Rapids with clear passages, but they may be through narrow spots, requiring expertise in maneuvering. Scouting may be necessary.

Class IV: Advanced. Long rapids; waves powerful and irregular; dangerous rocks and boiling eddies. Passages difficult to scout; powerful and precise maneuvering required. Scouting mandatory first time. Risk of overturning or wrapping boat, and long swims for paddlers. For very skilled boaters.

Class V: Expert. Extremely difficult, long, very violent rapids, following each other almost without interruption; riverbed extremely obstructed. Big drops; violent current; very steep gradient. Scouting mandatory but often difficult. Risk of boat damage and serious injury to paddlers. For teams of experts with excellent equipment.

Class VI: Extreme. Extraordinarily difficult. Extremes of navigability. Nearly impossible and very dangerous. For teams of experts only, at favorable water levels and after close study with all precautions.

Class V action. COURTESY OF MARK LISK/AIRE, INC.

A plus or minus sign is sometimes added to further fine-tune these classifications, for example, Class III+ or Class IV-.

Another rating system, known as the Western Scale, is occasionally used, appearing mostly on maps of some western rivers. This system rates rapids on a scale of 1 to 10. Some boaters prefer the Western Scale because it is more precise, but most river descriptions still use the International Scale exclusively.

Determining whether your skill level is adequate for the river's difficulty is imperative for safety. Keep in mind that rapids may be underrated. Experts, who are often rafters or hardshell kayakers, tend to underestimate minor rapids that may be challenging for an IK paddler.

Ratings can change quickly as well, especially when water levels are higher than normal. A straightforward Class III at a medium water level can easily become a Class V should the river rise. Note how the Western Scale ratings of rapids in Hells Canyon of the Snake River are affected by a changing river level:

Rapids	Low Water Level	High Water Level
Wildsheep	7	9
Waterspout	8	6
Sluice Creek	6	7
Wild Goose	5	5

In some cases, rising water makes the rapids more difficult; in others, even on the same river, the rapids become easier. Most are more difficult at higher levels, however, simply because the speed and force of the current are increased.

There are other considerations as well. A remote river requires a higher level of skill than one close to civilization. Cold water creates an additional hazard because of the possibility of hypothermia. A river with sharp rocks or strainers (where the river filters through downed trees or boulders) is more hazardous. Rapids without distinct routes are more difficult to navigate and more dangerous than those followed by long, quiet pools, which give a boater a chance to easily swim to shore if necessary. And

even in easy rapids, a strainer can make for a very dangerous situation.

Ratings should be regarded for what they are—general, subjective guidelines that may not always be accurate.

A less difficult, safe run.
CECIL KUHNE

THE TONGUE OF THE RAPIDS

The entrance to most rapids is marked by one or more V-shaped currents. These currents, called the tongue of the rapids, are very useful to boaters, as they usually indicate the best entry point into the whitewater that lies beyond.

When still water becomes white, the current is usually the fastest and deepest in the center. This is because friction occurring between the water and a shallow riverbed slows the current.

In deeper areas, the current is swifter and more powerful. This stronger current clears rocks away from the main channel, creating the characteristic V-shaped lead-in at the head of most rapids. This V usually points to the deepest and least obstructed channel. If there's more than one tongue, the best one will usually be the longest or the one that drops the most quickly.

But beware of the upstream V, where the tip of the V points upstream rather than down. This is a shock wave created by an obstruction just beneath the surface and is a warning to stay clear.

Tongue of the rapids. The tongue is usually used as a point of entry. The characteristic V-shaped lead-in at the head of most rapids usu-ally points to the deepest and least obstructed channel.

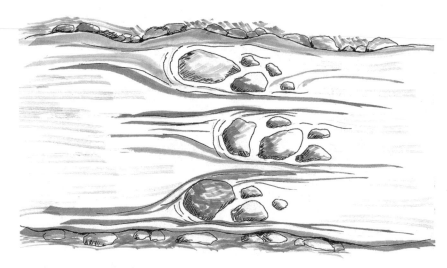

Running the V.
COURTESY OF MARK LISK/AIRE, INC.

REVERSALS

Rocks protruding above the surface of the river are easy to spot. But when water flows over the top of a rock and into the slack water behind it, the water creates a back-flow as it moves upstream and then back on itself. The movement of the current on the downstream side of a rock is known as a *reversal*. Reversals come in various shapes and sizes. If the rock is deeply submerged, a large reversal, known as a *hole*, may develop. The deeper the hole, the farther upstream the rock lies. Knowing the difference between friendly and not-so-friendly holes is the kayaker's most important skill.

Small holes present little trouble. But there are larger holes, called *stoppers*, that can stop—and even flip—a boat. Still larger ones, called *keepers*, can hold and recirculate a boat with ease.

How do you determine when a wave is a reversal? When the rock is barely underwater, it may be difficult to spot from upstream because little turbulence is created. Look for a calm spot in the midst of turbulence. Usually the rock will deflect the current, and as a result, the water will level out as it sweeps over the rock. Other rocks may be concealed by spray and can be seen only by steady observation. Viewing a reversal from shore often allows you to see rocks that aren't visible when you're on the river.

In a hole's extreme form—a waterfall—water plunges downward to the riverbed. Within the chaos is a jumble of violent currents. As the current comes back toward the surface and repeats the cycle, not much is allowed to escape, including a boat or boater caught inside.

Reversal. When water flows over the top of a rock and into the placid water behind it, a backflow is created as it moves upstream and then back upon itself. This movement of the current on the downstream side of a rock is known as a reversal.

STANDING WAVES

When fast currents slow down as the gradient of the river decreases, the water often starts to pile up. If the transition is gradual, there is turbulence in the form of *standing waves*. These are sometimes called *wave trains* or, if they're at the end of a stretch of rapids, *tail waves*. When standing waves converge, they surge randomly in a phenomenon known as *haystacks*.

While standing waves are found in most rapids, they are usually too small to cause concern. If the wave is high but gradual, it's best to approach it bow-first, allowing the boat to ride over the crest. Should your IK get tossed sideways, straighten out before the next wave if possible. If not, lean downstream and brace hard. If the waves are steep and angular and might overturn your boat, it's normally a good idea to move to the side, which is usually more gradual than the center.

It's best, however, to first make sure that the waves are, in fact, standing waves. Rocks just below the surface can create mounds of water that at first glance appear to be standing waves. Careful observation is required; standing waves are regular and patterned, while waves concealing submerged rocks are usually more jumbled.

PILLOWS

When the river's current collides with a rock, some of it forms an upstream mound, called a *pillow*. As the mound grows in size, it eventually spills over, creating a hydraulic. When the pillow deflects spray into the air, it's called a *roostertail*. Pillows should usually be avoided, because the rock or ledge they conceal may be undercut, allowing the current to plunge underneath. These can entrap a swimmer and are especially dangerous.

RECOGNIZING ROCKS

Huge boulders peeking above the surface of the water are obvious. Lower-lying rocks are more problematic. Hidden boulders just below the surface of the water are sometimes called *sleepers*. Watch for the characteristics that signal them. Water piles up on the upstream side of a rock, creating the *pillow*, which may or may not cover the rock entirely. Look, too, for *roostertails* shooting up above or behind a rock.

A haystack is exciting whitewater. COURTESY OF ORANGE TORPEDO TRIPS.

A series of waves tends to be regular in configuration, and rocks below the surface often upset the pattern. If the last wave in a series doesn't fit the pattern, a rock may be lying underneath. Look closely, too, into the white froth for a glimpse of darkness that may signal a rock.

BENDS

A river's tendency to meander causes the erosion of its banks. As this erosion continues, the current gradually carves out a new bend. The current then begins to pile up on the outside of the bend, while the inside of the bend becomes increasingly shallow.

The deepest and fastest current is usually found along the outside of the bend. The current has a tendency to move the boat to the outside of the bend, which often contains large boulders, overhanging trees, undercut cliffs, and other hazards. It's best, then, to first approach the rapids from the inside of the bend. Then, if the outside of the bend is free of impediments, it's easy to move to that side of the river

EDDIES

Eddies are currents that move upstream, behind rocks or projections along the bank. The term *eddy* is also used to refer to the slack water on the inside of a bend, even though it doesn't move upstream.

The imaginary line between the main current and the eddy is known as the *eddy fence*, or *eddy line*. Here the currents between the eddy and the main current mix and swirl. The eddy line can be very powerful, even capable of moving a boat back upstream.

Eddies are useful for boaters entering or leaving shore, and they can often be used to stop the boat in midstream. Some eddies, especially swirling whirlpools, should be avoided because they are capable of trapping a boat and rotating it for what seems indefinitely.

FERRYING

The technique for crossing a river to avoid obstacles is commonly known as *ferrying*. The simplest kind of ferry, the *downstream ferry*, uses the power of a river's current, along with a few forward strokes, to move the boat across the river. But there are times when it's better to use an *upstream ferry*, paddling against the current. The

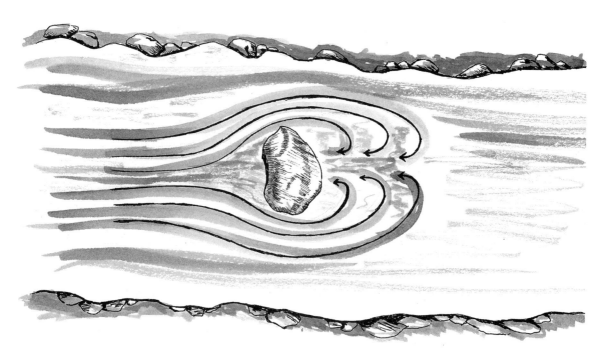

upstream ferry allows you to use the much more powerful forward stroke to slow your speed in the current. Paddling upstream counteracts the force of the current, while the boat's angle to the current helps you cross the river. The key to either the downstream or upstream ferry is the angle of the boat in relation to the current. The best ferry angle is usually 45 degrees or so, depending on the force of the current.

With the *back ferry*, the principle is the same as the downstream ferry, but the paddle stroke is reversed. Here you face the obstacle you want to avoid and backpaddle away from it. This technique allows you to see the hazards downstream and to slow your speed in the current while moving laterally across the current.

AVOIDING ROCKS AND OTHER OBSTACLES

It's best to anticipate upcoming rocks well in advance. If, however, you're about to broach on a rock and you can't avoid the collision, lean *toward* the rock; if you were to follow instinct and lean away from the rock, the IK could flip and become pinned against it. Fortunately, many boulders have a pillow on the upstream side, which tends to push you away from the rock.

An eddy is any current that runs contrary to the direction of the river's main flow. Eddies generally run upstream, either behind rocks in the river or projections along its banks.

On the outside bend of a river, currents tend to sweep boaters into cliff walls, large boulders, or downed trees. You need to anticipate this well in advance and begin correcting your course immediately. The back ferry is often the most effective technique in this situation, since it allows you to see downstream and to slow your course.

Some rivers have rapids strewn with rocks and boulders, known as *boulder gardens* or *rock gardens*. Scout these rapids before running them so that you can plan a careful route through them. Use the eddies that form behind the rocks to assist your turns or slow your boat down.

THE HIGHSIDE

On a moving river, you quickly learn about the boat's balance. One side of the inflatable kayak can be sucked down, causing the opposite side to rise upward. When this occurs, the upward side is called the *highside*. To avoid overturning, counteract this force by shifting your body weight *toward* the highside. Usually, just a quick *lean* toward the highside will restore stability. Never lean away from the highside, or you'll capsize. A quick brace or draw stroke may also help you to restore balance.

STRAINERS AND SWEEPERS

During spring floods, rivers can carry a lot of natural debris, including fallen trees, branches, and sticks wedged between rocks. River runners call these downed trees *strainers* and *sweepers* because they allow the current to pour through them but strain anything else, like boats and boaters, into their branches. With the force of the water moving into such obstacles, they can present extremely dangerous situations, so move to avoid strainers and sweepers well in advance. Also keep alert for logs pinned between rocks; with careful observation, you should be able to see them before you get too close.

SCOUTING RAPIDS

Always scout a stretch of rapids whose path you cannot see clearly from the river. Stay alert for the signs of major rapids ahead: noise, spray, an abrupt drop in the horizon line, a wall of boulders across a river, or a narrow gorge.

To scout rapids, stop and walk downstream to get a closer look at what's coming up. Look for obvious obstacles and routes around them. Walk the entire stretch of rapids from shore if it's one you're not familiar with or if the route isn't clear. It's much easier to spot hidden rocks and reversals from a downstream vantage point. Also check the end of the rapids to see where you'll be when you finish and to make certain there aren't more rapids below.

Look for prominent features to serve as mental markers of your course when you make the run. Identifying those markers is important because of the difference in your perspective. From a high vantage point, the correct path seems obvious, but when you start into the rapids, you'll find yourself in a confusing maze of rocks and foam.

After you've looked over the entire stretch of rapids and decided on a course, pause one last time at the top. A second look at the entry is always a good idea. If other boaters are coming through the rapids, watch them.

Depending on the configuration of the river, it may be necessary to scout from both shores. Boaters sometimes toss sticks into the river to better judge where certain currents will take their boats. Spend enough time scouting to become comfortable with your route. Always have an optional route in mind as well, just in case something should go wrong with your first choice.

RUNNING THE RAPIDS

You've had a long, close look at the rapids below, either from the boat or from the shore. You've finally decided on your route through the whitewater maze. Now it's time for the run—and some fun!

Entry. The entry into the rapids is the most critical maneuver of all. Selecting the proper entry into a stretch of rapids often determines the rest of the run. Many rapids, perhaps most, require little maneuvering if correctly entered. The rapids you are entering will no doubt appear different from your perspective on the water than when you were scouting them, so a last-minute look will be helpful. You may want to kneel in the boat for a better look. Once you've decided on your route, don't change your mind midstream unless you see something significant that you didn't spot earlier.

The basic rule for entry is to keep the boat headed directly into the waves of the rapids. This position is the most stable; a boat that's sideways to the current is more prone to overturning.

Navigating Holes. Knowing which holes to avoid is the essence of the art. Slowing your speed downstream is

Avoiding holes. CECIL KUHNE

essential; this is typically accomplished through a series of ferry maneuvers across the river, moving the boat along the deepest and least obstructed channels.

If there are holes you can't avoid, try to punch through them as hard and fast as you can. This maneuver takes advantage of the current flowing downstream of the hole. Throwing your weight downstream may also help you push through.

Navigating Bends. The ferry maneuver is especially important on bends in the river. Currents, unfortunately, don't curve with the river's bends. Instead, they flow in a straight line from the inside of the bend to the outside. As a result, the river's tendency is to propel a boat to the outside of the bend. To avoid this, you must enter the bend from the inside corner. It's easier to follow the current to the outside of the bend if the path is clear rather than to fight the current to the inside if it's not.

Eddies. In a stretch of violent whitewater, eddies can present havens of safety while you catch your breath or scout the rest of the rapids. The force of the current is stronger the farther you move upstream in the eddy. If you need to stop quickly, aim high in the eddy or you may miss it. Enter the eddy with a good angle and speed in order to pierce the eddy line, which is usually moving faster than the main current. Once you cross the eddy line, the upstream current will catch the boat. Eddies allow for amazingly dramatic stops and turns. To avoid tipping or even flipping the boat, do not enter or leave eddies too quickly.

Highsiding. If your boat becomes caught on rocks, you can usually free it by shifting your weight to the downstream side of the boat, which will then swing free. If the current is strong enough, however, the boat may keep sliding up the obstacle while the lower tube dives deeper into the current. Eventually the river will push the lower tube underneath and then pin the boat against the obstacle, causing a *wrap*.

To avoid a wrap, lean on the downstream tube (the one riding up on the rock); this is known as *highsiding*. This forces the tube down, causing the upstream tube to ride higher and allowing the current to pass underneath. The technique also works in a large hole. To avoid flipping, lean downstream to paddle or push the boat out of the hole.

Bouldering. Small boulders can provide convenient breaks in continuous whitewater. You can bring your boat to a halt by running it onto a partially submerged boulder, then spin it off the boulder to continue downstream.

Bailing. A boat without the self-bailing feature can accumulate an incredible amount of water, rendering it difficult to maneuver. On rivers with continuous whitewater, it's important to keep the boat bailed and therefore as light as possible.

SURFING WAVES

The art of *surfing* a river wave is much like riding an ocean swell, except that on a river, the waves are stationary and the water moves through them.

Look for waves that are regular in shape and evenly formed. Turn your boat to face upstream as you enter the waves, then paddle as hard as you can, straight upstream. When the boat stalls on a wave, you're surfing. A rudder stroke will keep the boat from slipping sideways.

Some paddlers prefer to surf their boats while kneeling rather than sitting. This position provides more

Surfing a wave. COURTESY OF
MARK LISK/AIRE, INC.

power, as well as more excitement for the paddler. If you kneel, however, your center of gravity is higher, which can throw you off balance.

LOW-WATER TECHNIQUE

Besides extending the boating season, low-water kayaking offers greater opportunities for solitude, because bigger boats are unable to attempt such runs.

The river is generally less intimidating at lower water levels. There may be more obstacles to avoid, but the river is moving more slowly, allowing additional time for scouting rapids and making decisions. Less volume means reduced power as well, so the river may be more forgiving.

On the other hand, at lower levels, some rapids will have to be lined or portaged because there won't be enough water to maneuver. Constant rock-dodging can be tiring. A short, narrow IK fits better into tight slots and turns more quickly than a broader, longer IK. Load the IK light so that it will be more maneuverable and easier to float over shallows.

To avoid the frustration of coming to a halt in every shallow spot, keep looking ahead for signs of shoals. If the river is clear, a color change alone may alert you to shallows. Watch the surface of the river and follow the waves. River current favors the high bank and the outside of bends.

HIGH-WATER TECHNIQUE

Large rapids demand special skills; don't attempt large-volume rivers until you're ready for them. The main problem with high water is the incredible force of the current. You'll need to scout big-water rapids very carefully from shore. If the water's cold, wear protective clothing.

Once on the river, paddle hard into the big waves so that the kayak doesn't slide backward. If you get knocked sideways by a powerful wave, correct your position immediately so that the IK doesn't flip. Keep a lookout for eddies, especially when scouting big rapids. They offer safe landing places, temporary havens from the rapids.

IKs that don't self-bail may have difficulty maneuvering after becoming swamped by big waves. The quickest way to empty an IK is to land the boat, climb out, and turn it upside down. If you can't get to shore and there are no eddies in sight, bailing may be difficult, especially if the next stretch of rapids is just downstream.

The greatest danger in high water comes from reversals, which swell to enormous proportions. If you find yourself in a large hole, head in bow-first and paddle furiously. You need to generate enough speed to push through the wave and power your boat out of the hole.

Should you lose momentum, you'll feel the kayak sliding backward. Brace hard downstream to keep the kayak upright. You may be able to catch the current below the surface with your paddle and then propel the IK free. If you're caught in such a situation, don't panic. The recirculating effect ends at the sides of the reversal, so try to work your way to one side if you can. If this fails, thrust your paddle below the surface to reach the forward-flowing current.

What about waterfalls? You may have seen photographs of kayaks jumping falls, but this is not recommended. Even experts have suffered neck injuries, leaving them quadriplegics for life. It's simply not worth the risk.

8

RIVER SAFETY

Unless you've actually been there, it's difficult to imagine the force of a river pounding down on a boat out of control. Like many pursuits, whitewater boating can be dangerous. But it's also true that the sport's dangers have been greatly exaggerated by the media. Most river accidents can be prevented with a little foresight and caution. Also, most river accidents don't happen on the river, but in camp. And the consequences of any accident are made more serious by remoteness.

PERSONAL PREPARATION
The best safety measures are preventive. Sharpening wilderness skills, staying in shape, keeping equipment in good repair, and researching the territory you plan to cover are all important. Still, accidents do happen, even to the most experienced, so you should always be prepared for possible problems. It's also important to know the proper procedures for rescuing boaters and boats.

It's always a good idea to start on easy rivers early in the season and gain some experience before moving on to more difficult water. When running any river you're not familiar with, get all the information you can, from guide-

Always scout unknown rapids ahead. CECIL KUHNE

books, maps, magazine articles, and other boaters. On the river, try to maintain a fairly relaxed pace, and allow plenty of time for scouting or lining rapids.

GROUP TRAVEL

Most kayakers travel in groups of two or more for greater safety. When traveling in a group, there are always other people to assist in the rescue of boaters and boats if an emergency should develop. The most experienced boater should lead the group, determining the best route through each stretch of rapids and waiting below as the rest of the paddlers come through. Another experienced boater should run as a sweep boat behind the group to make sure that everyone makes it safely through the run and nobody gets left behind. Inexperienced boaters should never pass the lead boat. Each boater should keep the one behind him in sight at all times.

Although at times they may travel close together, boaters should increase the distance between each other while running rapids. Crowding together not only

Experienced kayakers should paddle the lead and sweep boats in a group.
COURTESY OF ORANGE TORPEDO TRIPS.

restricts maneuverability, but also increases the chance of collision or of forcing a boat against an obstacle in the river. There should be sufficient distance between boats that if the first boater sees trouble, he can stop immediately. Each boater, after running the rapids, can establish a position for the rescue of those following if necessary.

Signals. When traveling in groups, a set of hand or paddle signals, agreed upon at the beginning of the trip, can be helpful in communicating, especially when there is some distance between boats and the roar of rapids makes verbal communication impossible.

Signals should be simple: hand or paddle outstretched horizontally for "stop"; a waved hand or paddle for "help"; and a hand or paddle outstretched vertically for "all clear."

Rescue Stations. In dangerous whitewater, position a couple of boaters with throw ropes at key points along the rapids to render assistance if needed. Stationing rescuers downstream from where a flip might occur will give a swimmer time to get to the surface of the water and clear his vision so that he can spot the rescue rope being thrown to him.

Responsibilities of the Group Leader. If you lead a trip, you have special responsibilities. You need to get the appropriate maps and guidebooks, together with detailed information about the rapids. Find out whether the river level is above or below normal and, if so, how it will affect the run. Determine points of possible assistance along your route in case of emergency. Review with the other boaters all safety and rescue matters: hazards downstream, the locations of rescue stations, the order in which the group should travel, and signals.

Before beginning the trip, notify the appropriate authorities of your trip plans in case rescue will be needed. Before embarking on a long or remote trip, let someone back home know so that he can send a search party if you're overdue. It is also the leader's responsibility to check *all* gear—life jackets, rescue rope, first-aid kit, repair materials, and survival equipment.

EQUIPMENT PRECAUTIONS

Your boat must be in good working order, even more important on remote rivers. For unfamiliar rivers, make

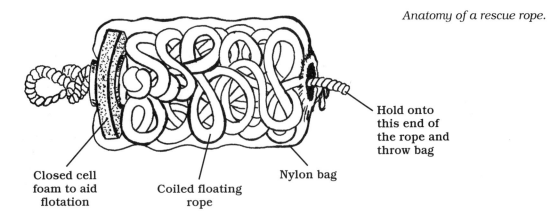

Anatomy of a rescue rope.

Hold onto
this end of
the rope and
throw bag

Closed cell
foam to aid
flotation

Coiled floating
rope

Nylon bag

certain that your boat and equipment are of adequate size and quality for the water you plan to run.

The most indispensable piece of safety equipment is your life jacket, or PFD. Make sure it provides sufficient flotation for the whitewater you will be tackling.

Rig your boat properly. Eliminate any sharp projections that could possibly cause injury. Check that nothing will cause entanglement if the boat should overturn. If your boat is not a self-bailer or catamaran, carry a good bailing bucket, and make sure it's secured to the boat.

Take plenty of rope in case rescue is necessary. On difficult rivers, you should have at least 100 feet of rope for boat rescue in addition to what you ordinarily use for bow and stern lines. Carabiners also come in handy. For rescuing boaters, rescue ropes made for that purpose are excellent because they float and can be easily tossed.

You also need to carry a repair kit that includes repair materials not only for your boat, but also for other equipment, such as paddle and air pump.

EMERGENCY GEAR

Carry basic emergency gear and know how to use it. Each IK should carry a throw bag for rescuing swimmers or pulling boats off rocks. The group's gear should include a spare breakdown paddle and at least two air pumps, in case one is lost or breaks down. The party also needs a good repair kit and a first-aid kit (see appendix for complete lists). Each paddler, especially in cold weather or wilderness situations, should carry some kind of survival kit on his person, with a fire starter, waterproof matches, a rescue carabiner, and a signal whistle. Most kayakers carry knives attached to their PFDs to cut themselves free from entangling ropes.

CLOTHING

Always wear adequate clothing to protect against cold water and sunburn. Wear protective footgear, a helmet on rocky rivers, a wetsuit or drysuit on cold rivers, sunglasses and a hat to cut down on glare and improve your view, and eyeglass retainers to prevent loss.

HYPOTHERMIA

Hypothermia is a lowering of body temperature to a dangerous level. Any boater exposed to cold weather, and especially cold water, can become a victim. Symptoms of hypothermia typically include fatigue, apathy, forgetfulness, and confusion. Shivering may or may not occur. In near-freezing water, the time from immersion to death can be as short as ten minutes.

Awareness of the causes of hypothermia and the speed with which death can result is the most important aspect of prevention.

Treatment is fairly simple, and the sooner, the better. First, replace wet clothes with dry ones. Then move the person into a warm shelter. If he is unable to generate his own body heat, rewarming is required.

Heat from a supplemental source should be provided. Build a fire or, if that's not possible, use body heat from others (lightly clothed for best results). Hot liquids may also help, but *never* give them alcoholic drinks, which dilate the blood vessels and cause even greater heat loss. If the person becomes unconscious, the situation is extremely serious, and he must be hospitalized as soon as possible.

Hypothermia can be prevented, to a large extent, by adequate clothing, proper food, and good physical conditioning. The best protection is a wetsuit or drysuit, although if you dump in very cold water, get out immediately, even if this means abandoning your boat to swim for shore. Even with protective clothing, hypothermia can set in quickly. The food you eat is also important; sugar and carbohydrates are quickly oxidized by the body to provide heat and energy. It also pays to stay in shape, as a physically fit boater is less susceptible to hypothermia.

HYPOTHERMIA SYMPTOMS

99–96 degrees F.	The body usually starts to shiver uncontrollably. The victim cannot do complex tasks.
95–91 degrees F.	Usually, the victim still shivers violently. He has trouble speaking clearly.
90–86 degrees F.	Shivering decreases or stops, and the victim cannot think clearly. The muscles are stiff but the victim keeps his posture. Total amnesia may occur. The victim usually can keep in psychological contact with the environment.
85–81 degrees F.	The victim becomes irrational, loses contact with environment, and drifts into stupor.
80–78 degrees F.	The victim becomes unconscious and does not respond to the spoken word. His heartbeat becomes irregular, and there are no reflexes.
below 78 degrees F.	Death occurs as the result of complications arising from failure of the cardiac and respiratory centers in the brain. These may include cardiac fibrillation and pulmonary edema. There is hemorrhage in the lungs.

You may need to paddle ashore to turn a capsized boat upright. CECIL KUHNE

SELF-RESCUE

In case you should go overboard, it is important that you know how to perform a self-rescue. First of all, there may be no one else around. And even if there are other paddlers nearby, it's easier and faster for you to rescue yourself than to depend on someone else.

First, don't panic. Hold on to your paddle, if you can, because you're going to need it once you're back in the boat. Next, look for your boat. In most cases, it'll be right next to you.

Now, this is where handholds and flip lines (or straps) come into play. The bottom of the IK will be smooth and slippery, and therefore difficult to hold. Short grab loops or big D-rings at bow and stern offer good handholds, and a flip line fastened around the IK is even better.

Once you grab the IK, you need to turn it upright. A pull on the flip line will accomplish this quickly. If the boat is empty, it'll be easy to turn over in the middle of the river; if you have a heavy load, you may have to swim the boat to shore or into an eddy.

Getting back into the upright boat is a matter of pulling yourself over the tubes. Put the paddle inside first. Approach the IK from the upstream side, to avoid being pinned between it and a rock. Reach across the IK and pull yourself back in with the help of the flip line.

If you can't get back into the IK, pull it to shore, keeping the boat downstream of you so that there's no chance of your becoming wedged between it and a rock.

Swimming in Whitewater. Every paddler should know how to swim safely through whitewater. The basic safety rules are as follows:

- Hold on to your paddle if you can, and get to the boat's upstream end. A boat full of water can otherwise pin you against an obstruction. Try to get back into the boat.
- Let go of your boat or any other gear if it drags you into a dangerous situation.
- If you can't get back into the boat, float on your back with your feet held high and pointed downstream. That way, your feet, not your head, will meet any obstruction first. Backpaddle with your arms for control.
- Take a breath as you are carried into the trough of the wave. When the current lifts you to the crest,

Swimming rapids. The correct swimming posture is important to reduce the chance of injury. The feet are headed downstream to push off rocks and other obstacles until a safe landing place is found.

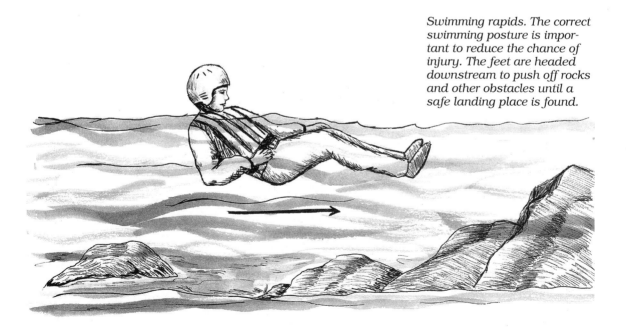

hold your breath. Depending on how large it is, the wave will probably come crashing over your head, inhibiting breathing for a few seconds.

- Stay with the boat if possible until you get your strength and can see a safe place to land. Then swim to shore as quickly as possible, taking the boat with you if you can do so without danger.
- If you're about to be swept into a fallen tree, face forward and try to climb up onto it so that you aren't swept underneath and trapped.
- If you're headed for a big drop, tuck into a ball. This will protect your body if you hit the riverbottom.
- Don't try to stand up in a moving current, even if the water is shallow, because it can easily knock you over. Your feet could then become pinned under a rock, and if the current pushes your head underwater, you can drown in a few feet of water.

Avoiding Entrapment. The combination of a river current and an entangling object can prove fatal. Boaters on moving water must be alert for possible entrapment situations, including loose ropes, logs, and undercut rocks in swift currents.

Never tie yourself into a boat on moving water. When being rescued by a throw line or when swimming white-water, never wrap or tie a rope around any part of your body. Keep all lines on your boat secured, and have cargo tied down with straps that are just long enough to do the job, without any extra length hanging loose. Carry a survival knife on your PFD in order to cut any entangling ropes.

Some of the worst hazards of a river are currents that flow through overhanging trees (called *sweepers*) or through downed trees or boulders (called *strainers*). If a collision with a strainer or sweeper is inevitable, approach it headfirst, and the moment before you hit it, kick with your legs and try to pull your body over it. Do anything you can to avoid entrapment.

Recirculating holes are another entrapment hazard. Most holes are too small to be keepers. If you aren't flushed out immediately, try to swim sideways out of the hole. Large holes can recirculate a swimmer almost indefinitely. Here, the best way to escape the force is to reach the powerful downcurrent. You can do this by tucking yourself into a cannonball position (to avoid injury when you hit the riverbed), and then, after you hit the riverbed, swim hard to reach the deep currents moving downstream.

RESCUE OF OTHERS

All river runners need to know the proper techniques for the rescue of boaters and boats. I strongly recommend reading the books *River Rescue*, by Les Bechdel and Slim Ray, and *Whitewater Rescue Manual*, by Charles Walbridge and Wayne Sundmacher.

When running rivers with powerful currents, it is always advisable to have safety lines downstream for the rescue of those who may be unable to swim ashore. A number of lines made specially for rescue are now available. These lines come in nylon bags with one end of the line attached to the bottom of the bag. You simply hold the end of the line and throw the entire bag, which feeds out like a spinning reel. On the second throw, the rescue line is coiled. Half of the coil is held in one hand and half in the other. The first coil is thrown with an underhanded motion, while the second is allowed to feed out freely, with the remaining end held securely in hand.

First, make sure that the rescue path is free of strainers, sweepers, boulder gardens, and other hazards. Throw the line slightly downstream from the swimmer, since he is moving along with the current. After he grabs the rescue line, a tremendous pull will be exerted on the line. The rescuer should then belay the line around a tree or around his waist.

After the swimmer grabs the rope, he should turn on his back, face up. This allows his body to plane toward the surface and offers less resistance. He should *never* wrap the rope around any part of his body, for safety reasons.

The best rescue boat is a raft, but one is not always available. Another IK paddler may help, but he should use caution; an overeager victim leaping onto the middle of an IK can throw the boat off balance. The best approach is to have the victim hold on to the stern of the boat without getting in, or lie over its tubes, keeping his weight low.

RESCUE OF BOATS

In shallow rivers, your kayak may become lodged on a rock or gravel bar, and it's normally easy to simply push it off the obstacle. But if the boat should collide with large boulders that protrude above the river's surface, a more serious situation may occur.

If your kayak is headed toward a large boulder, it is usually best to strike it with the bow of the boat. That way, the current of the river, with the aid of a few paddling strokes, will invariably swing the boat off the rock.

A sideways collision with a rock is more problematic. If this situation, known as *pinning*, seems unavoidable, you may still be able to prevent it by leaning toward the downstream side of the boat, which lifts the upstream tube out of the water, allowing the current to flow underneath. Be wary of entrapment, and prepare to abandon the boat if necessary.

If the boat does become pinned against a rock, attempt to free it by the following methods: First, shift your weight to the side of the boat most likely to spin off the rock. It may even be possible to then manually push the boat away from the rock. If that fails, try placing the paddle into the main flow of the river to catch the force of the current and pull the boat off the rock. If these methods fail, you'll have to attach lines to the boat and pull from shore.

If the kayak's upstream tube is pulled completely underwater, a more serious situation, known as *wrapping* the boat, presents itself. If the kayak is wrapped on a large rock, but not too seriously, you may be able to stand on the rock and pull the boat up and out of the water. If this isn't possible, or if it doesn't succeed, you'll have to attach lines to several points on the kayak's bow and stern and then pull with all your might from shore.

This is where mechanical engineering comes into play. A variety of intricate retrieval systems (beyond the scope of this book) have been developed by professionals to utilize mechanical advantages. See the book *River Rescue*, mentioned earlier in this chapter, for details.

If you are still not able to unwrap the boat, it may help to deflate the section of the kayak that is under the greatest stress and then pull on the inflated section. This often reduces much of the pressure and weight of the water, though unfortunately it can also cause the boat to wrap more tightly to the rock. If all else fails, you may have to abandon the boat, after first securing it to shore, until lower water levels allow easier access.

LINING AND PORTAGING

Never boat water beyond your ability. When faced with a stretch of rapids that appears too tough, and you decide not to run it, you have two options: You can carry the boat around the rapids, known as a *portage*, or you can guide the boat down the bank with ropes, called *lining*. Lining is easier, but it takes practice to be able to control the boat from shore.

Before lining, first lash down or remove all the gear. Attach two lines to the IK, one on the bow and one on the stern. It's easier for two people to do the lining. The person with the bow line leads the boat downriver, while the person with the stern line pays out the rope slowly, acting as brake and anchor to keep the IK from getting out of control.

In rocky stretches of the river, lining is difficult because of tight maneuvering. In shallow areas, it's often necessary to have someone push the boat along or move it farther into the current, while others maintain control with lines attached to the boat. In sections of the river with powerful currents and no obstructions, the boat can be allowed to float freely—with lines attached but slackened—to the calm water below.

When lining a boat, always wear your life jacket.

GETTING HELP IN EMERGENCIES

If, despite preventative measures, a serious injury does occur on the river, remain calm and treat the injured person to the best of your ability. If you're close to civilization, someone may be able to walk to the nearest road. If there are other paddlers on the river, ask them to go for help.

PRESERVING OUR RIVERS

It's a sad fact of life, but our rivers are in peril—and the attacks on them come from many sides. Pollution claims a number of rivers. Urbanization destroys many others. Dams continue to be built in the name of progress, however ill-defined. In the process, free-flowing streams are being eradicated from the face of the earth forever.

On those rivers that have been spared, boaters are sometimes accused of loving them to death. Overuse of what is surely nature's greatest resource makes it imperative that we take care of what we have left.

TRACELESS CAMPING

In the total scheme of things, what difference does one candy bar wrapper make? The answer is *a lot*, when the single effect is multiplied a thousandfold, as it invariably is.

A study by the National Park Service looked at the impact of river runners in the Grand Canyon. Here's what they found:

- Human debris, such as food, plastic, and other trash, is accumulating on the riverbanks at rates that exceed the purging capacities of natural processes.

Away from crowds. COURTESY OF LEON WERDINGER/JACK'S PLASTIC WELDING.

- Live, standing trees are being used for firewood.
- Ash and charcoal from campfires are spread into the ground at rates that far surpass nature's ability to clean the soil.
- More than 20 tons of human waste are produced by those traveling through the Grand Canyon. Under previous park policy, some five thousand human waste burial sites were dug along the river. Present regulations require all human waste to be carried out.
- Campsites are drastically overused. Fewer than one hundred campsites receive more than 75 percent of all use by the fifteen thousand who float the river each year. At some sites, thirty or forty people camp every night during the busiest four months of the year.

Garbage Disposal. The rule for disposal of garbage is simple: carry it *all* out. The best method for doing this is to take along a plastic bucket with an airtight lid (fast-food chains use them for pickles and mustard and will usually give them away) or a heavy-duty plastic bag placed in a more resilient nylon bag. Keep a small bag handy for use during the day, and be careful to collect all cigarette butts and other small debris.

If using a campfire or charcoal briquets, burn all trash possible. Certain foods, such as eggshells, require more than a just a short morning fire to be totally burned. If you have garbage that cannot be burned, such as aluminum foil packets, dispose of it by placing everything except liquids in the garbage bag. Strain all liquid garbage, such as coffee, soup, or dishwater, and throw the strained-out solids into the garbage bag. In wooded areas, the liquid residue should be poured on the ground, at least 100 feet from any area normally used for camping. In the desert, where decomposition is slower, the liquid should be poured into the main current of the river. Grease, however, should always be carried out.

Human Waste Disposal. Solid human waste presents an environmental impact and a hazard to human health. Many river management agencies require that all solid human waste be carried out of the river corridor. It's inevitable that the system will soon be implemented on most government lands, and it's a good idea in all heavily traveled areas.

The system is easy to set up. A military surplus ammunition box (sometimes called a rocket box) serves as the toilet container, and a toilet seat is placed on top. A small amount of a chemical deodorant is then poured into the box. Chemical deodorants are important because they reduce bacterial growth and the production of methane gas. A water dispenser and hand soap should be placed nearby.

Side hikes also require sanitary waste disposal, but of a slightly different kind. To reduce impact, carefully burn the toilet paper, then bury the waste in a hole about 6 inches deep—the best depth for rapid decomposition. Carry a small backpacker's trowel for this purpose, and make the hole at least 100 feet from the river's high-water line and any camping areas.

THE NATIONAL WILD AND SCENIC RIVERS ACT

The Environmental Protection Agency once tried to tally the number of dams on America's rivers, but they lost count somewhere around sixty thousand. In our rush to

The National Wild and Scenic Rivers Act protects rivers from being dammed and controls development of the river corridor. CECIL KUHNE

reap the benefits of dams, some 600,000 miles of river have been drowned behind concrete and steel. As a result, the wild character of rivers has been sacrificed in the name of progress.

Only recently have we become concerned with the fate of our rivers. In 1968 the National Wild and Scenic Rivers Act was enacted to protect our rivers and highlight the importance of rivers over dams. How well has it worked? There are now more than 10,000 miles of rivers that are protected by the National Wild and Scenic Rivers System. It sounds impressive, but unfortunately, it's not even half of 1 percent of America's 3.5 million miles of rivers. For each mile of river preserved, 85 miles have been lost to dams.

But consider the alternative were the act not in place. There have been many significant achievements, and with the help of river runners, the future looks very bright indeed.

The concept of a system to save rivers began in the early sixties, when several Congressional committees endorsed the idea of a law to counterbalance the national agenda encouraging dams. As usual, however, it took years to work out the details of the act.

The act protects rivers by classifying them as wild, scenic, or recreational. It's a form of zoning that focuses on sustaining the wildness of the backcountry. The act recognizes that certain rivers possess such outstanding attributes—of scenery, recreation, geology, fish, wildlife, history, or culture—that they be kept free-flowing for all time.

But classifications, however important, are secondary to the real purpose of the act: to check damming. And the act goes even further by allowing managers to control development of the river corridor, either through outright purchase or through scenic easements.

Initially, protection was granted to sections of eight rivers: the Rogue, the Middle Fork of the Salmon, the Clearwater, the Rio Grande, the Wolf, the St. Croix, the Eleven Point, and the Feather. During the first ten years, only eight more rivers were added.

The act came too late for a number of outstanding rivers. The Tennessee River Valley has more miles of reservoir shoreline than all five Great Lakes. All but 149 of the 2,446 miles of the Missouri River have been dammed, and those 149 miles would have been too if not for the act. The Colorado River has been impounded to such an extent that, with the exception of local floods, none of its water has reached the Pacific in twenty-five years. The Columbia has been reduced to a succession of reservoirs, with little moving water in between.

Almost all the free-flowing rivers of California's Sierras have been dammed. A magnificent stretch of the Dolores in Colorado has been sacrificed in the name of irrigation water so expensive no farmer can afford it. Glen Canyon, which contains perhaps the most beautiful sandstone labyrinths in the world, now lies underneath Lake Powell, where you'd need scuba equipment to enjoy it. And the list goes on.

In 1980, the largest number of rivers—a total of twenty-six—were added in a single year, all Alaskan. President Carter, who made no friends of the dam lobby when he threatened to put the Army Corps of Engineers out of business, saw this as one of his greatest achievements.

With the election of Ronald Reagan as president, it was feared that progress would be halted. But the Reagan Administration was more amenable than expected,

The Grand Canyon's Colorado River. CECIL KUHNE

though not without some prodding. In Reagan's first four years, not one river was included, but eventually twenty-five rivers were added, most in 1987.

With the Bush Administration, things improved considerably. The number of river segments protected almost doubled, to the present total of 150 or so, which brings the average number of rivers protected every year since 1968 to only six.

There have been notable successes, and more than 10,000 miles of river have been saved. But much remains to be done. A long list of rivers has been identified by Congress as potential additions, but the process is slow. *As a result, the rate of river mileage lost is seventy-five times greater than the rate of river preservation.*

Only a minority of states have programs to protect rivers. And even on state-protected rivers, the Federal Energy Regulatory Commission (FERC) can override the designation, making it imperative that those rivers be added to the federal system.

In the meantime, several conservation groups are pursuing private pacts with federal agencies and corporations to buy some time. The Nature Conservancy has spent millions of dollars to purchase land for preservation along rivers, and American Rivers has secured years of protection through agreements with the Forest Service and the forest products industry. The American public is having some impact on the lawmakers as well.

THE FUTURE

Arguably, some dams do provide benefits that can't be obtained in other ways: irrigation, domestic water supplies, flood control, and hydroelectric power. But where do we draw the line? As former Secretary of the Interior Cecil Andrus says, "Streams and rivers have other values than just for electric power generation and irrigation and transportation. We need free-flowing water left in the nation for many reasons—including the protection of certain forms of life, for recreation, for scenic values, for maintenance of the tenuous link between modern man and his natural world."

In his book *Time and the River Flowing,* Francois Leydet points out the dilemma: "I suppose if we accept as a national policy that every resource of the country must be developed to the limit to support the greatest possible

Worth saving. CECIL KUHNE

human population, then we should right now give up the fight to save any untouched vestiges of our natural heritage. All rivers must be dammed, to prevent their wasting water into the ocean, and the consequent destruction of the beauty of natural rivers must be shrugged off as one of the prices of progress."

If we decide, instead, that rivers are worth saving, then before another dam is built, its necessity should be proven to be so overwhelming that no other reasonable alternative exists. The burden should be placed on those advocating change, not those supporting the status quo: a river in its natural state.

Otherwise, the consequences for all of us are too great to ignore. Because no force of nature affects the human spirit quite like running water. And with few exceptions, no amount of progress can be worth the loss of a river flowing free.

CHECKLISTS

DAY TRIPS
Inflatable kayak
Paddle
PFD
Helmet
Pump
Throw rope
Repair kit
First-aid kit
Bail bucket (if necessary)
Lunch
Water bottle
Sunscreen
Spare clothing in waterproof bag
Dry bag
Throwbag or rescue gear
River clothing suitable for conditions
Footgear
Camera
Map
Guidebook
Matches and fire starter
Toilet paper
Wallet and keys

OVERNIGHT TRIPS
All of the equipment listed for day trips plus the following:

Spare paddle
Full repair kit
Full first-aid kit
Emergency supplies, including space
    blankets
Camp clothing
Camp shoes
Carabiner or pulleys for rescues
Waterproof bags and boxes
Garbage bags
Tent or bivy shelter
Sleeping bag
Air mattress or pad
Food
Cookware, kitchen gear, and camp
    stove
Fuel
Flashlight
Water containers
Fire pan
Plastic trowel, folding shovel, or
    toilet box
Insect repellent
Toiletries
Signaling devices
Camera
Fishing gear, if desired

REPAIR KIT
Patching material
Adhesive
Solvent/thinner/cleaner
Small brush (for applying adhesive)
Scuffing tool/sandpaper
Rolling tool (for rolling down patches)
Scissors
Duct tape
Epoxy glue
Silicone rubber sealant
Bailing wire
Spare parts (valves, D-rings, etc.)

FIRST-AID KIT
Adhesive compress
Gauze pads
Gauze roller bandage
Triangular bandages
Burn ointment/spray
Antiseptic
Aspirin
Eye dressing kit
Tourniquet
Scissors
Tweezers
Cotton swabs
Snakebite kit
Adhesive tape
Band-aids
Splints
Ammonia inhalants
Sunburn lotion
Ace bandage
Butterfly closures
Razor blades
Safety pins
Moleskin
Salt tablets
Oil of cloves
Visine/Murine
Antiseptic towlettes
Calamine lotion
Antihistamine
Syrup of ipecac
Antacid

APPENDIX II

REFERENCES

BOOKS

Penny, Richard. *The Whitewater Source-book*. Birmingham, AL: Menasha Ridge Press, 1991.

Cassady, Jim, Bill Cross, and Fryar Calhoun. *Western Whitewater: From the Rockies to the Pacific*. Berkeley, CA: North Fork Press, 1994.

Ziegler, Ronald. *Wilderness Waterways: The Whole Water Reference for Paddlers*. Kirkland, WA: Canoe America Association, 1991.

MAGAZINES

American Whitewater
American Whitewater Association
P.O. Box 85
Phoenicia, NY 12464

Canoe & Kayak Magazine
Canoe America Associates
P.O. Box 3146
Kirkland, WA 98083
800-692-2663
206-827-6363

Currents
National Organization for River Sports
P.O. Box 6847
Colorado Springs, CO 80904
719-473-2466

Paddler
The Paddling Group
P.O. Box 1341
Eagle, ID 83616
800-752-7951
208-939-4500

INFLATABLE KAYAK MANUFACTURERS AND DISTRIBUTORS

AIRE, Inc.
P.O. Box 3412
Boise, ID 83703
208-344-7506

All River Equipment, Inc.
    (Star Inflatables brand)
232 Banks Rd.
Travelers Rest, SC 29690
803-836-2800

B&A Distributing
    (Riken and Momentum brands)
201 S.E. Oak St.
Portland, OR 97214
503-230-0482

Custom Inflatables
P.O. Box 80
Albright, WV 26519
800-673-3537
304-329-2359

Demaree Inflatable Boats, Inc.
P.O. Box 307
Friendsville, MD 21531
800-342-8823
301-746-5815

Duckworks
P.O. Box 100
Rowlesburg, WV 26425
800-872-7238
304-454-2473

ERC Manufacturing, Inc.
    (Wing Inflatables brand)
P.O. Box 279
Arcata, CA 95521
707-826-2887

Harmon-Incept Industries, Inc.
    (Incept brand)
3347 Hwy. 8 East, #7
Moscow, ID 83843
208-882-2844

Grabner Inflatables
9702 Gayton Rd., Suite 153
Richmond, VA 23233
800-360-2365
804-257-4166

Harrison Hoge Industries, Inc.
    (Sea Eagle brand)
200 Wilson St.
Port Jefferson Station, NJ 11776
800-852-0925
516-473-7308

Hyside Inflatables
P.O. Box Z
Kernville, CA 93238
800-868-5987
619-376-3723

Innova
7900 S.E. 28th, Suite 405
Mercer Island, WA 98040
206-669-7634

Jack's Plastic Welding, Inc.
115 S. Main
Aztec, NM 87410
505-334-8748

Jumbo Inflatables
1931 S.W. 14th St., #3
Portland, OR 97201
503-274-2313

Maravia Corporation
P.O. Box 404
Boise, ID 83701
800-867-7238
208-322-4949

Sevylor U.S.A. (Tahiti brand)
6651 E. 26th St.
Los Angeles, CA 90040
800-821-4645
213-727-6013

SOAR Inflatables
3152 Cherokee St.
St. Louis, MO 63103
800-280-7627
314-776-6994

Vista Recreation
85 Dills Rd.
Bryson City, NC 28713
704-488-8594

Water Wolf
P.O. Box 3341
Telluride, CO 81435
800-358-3169
970-728-3861

Whitewater Manufacturing (Sotar brand)
1700 S.W. Nebraska Ave.
Grants Pass, OR 97527
503-476-1344

Appendix IV

Equipment Sources

The Boat People
Inflatable Kayak Specialists
1249 South First St.
San Jose, CA 95110
408-258-7971

Carlisle Paddles, Inc.
P.O. Box 488
Grayling, MI 49738
800-258-0290
517-348-9886

Cascade Outfitters
P.O. Box 209
Springfield, OR 97477
800-223-7238
503-747-2272

Colorado Kayak Supply
P.O. Box 3059
Buena Vista, CO 81211
800-535-3565
719-395-2422

Down River Equipment
12100 West Sand Ave.
Wheat Ridge, CO 80033
303-467-9489

Four Corners River Sports
P.O. Box 379
Durango, CO 81302
800-426-7637
970-259-3893

NOC Outfitter's Store
13077 Hwy. 19 West
Bryson City, NC 28713
800-367-3521
704-488-6737

Northwest River Supplies
2009 S. Maine
Moscow, ID 83843
800-635-5202
208-882-2383

Pacific River Supply
3675 San Pablo Dam Rd.
El Sobrante, CA 94803
510-223-3675

Wyoming River Raiders
601 Wyoming Blvd.
Casper, WY 82609
800-247-6068
307-235-8624

COMMERCIAL OUTFITTERS

ACE Whitewater
P.O. Box 1168
Oak Hill, WV 25901
800-787-3982

Adventure Bound, Inc.
2392 H Rd.
Grand Junction, CO 81505
800-245-4668
303-245-5428

American River Touring Association
(ARTA)
24000 Casa Loma Rd.
Groveland, CA 95321
800-323-2782
209-962-7873

Holiday River Expeditions
544 East 3900 South
Salt Lake City, UT 84107
800-554-7238
801-266-2087

Kern River Tours
P.O. Box 3444
Lake Isabella, CA 93240
619-379-4616

Mountain River Tours
P.O. Box 88
Hico, WV 25854
800-822-1386
304-658-5266

Nantahala Outdoor Center
13077 Hwy. 19 W.
Bryson City, NC 28713
800-488-2175

New England Whitewater Center
P.O. Box 21
Caratunk, ME 04925
800-766-7238
207-672-5506

North American River Runners, Inc.
P.O. Box 81
Hico, WV 25854
800-950-2585
800-370-7238
304-658-5276

Northern Outdoors
P.O. Box 100
The Forks, ME 04985
207-663-4466

O.A.R.S.
P.O. Box 67
Angels Camp, CA 95222
800-346-6277
209-736-4677

Orange Torpedo Trips, Inc.
P.O. Box 1111
Grants Pass, OR 97526
800-635-2925
503-479-5061
503-479-2455

Professional Paddlesports Association
P.O. Box 248
Butler, KY 41006
606-472-2205

Rocky Mountain River Tours
P.O. Box 2552
Boise, ID 83701
208-345-2400

For information on other outfitters offering inflatable kayak trips, contact America Outdoors, P.O. Box 1348, Knoxville, TN 37901, 605-524-4814.

Paddling Clubs

Adobe Whitewater Club of New Mexico
P.O. Box 3835
Albuquerque, NM 87190

Adventure Whitewater Club
1550 North Ave.
Grand Junction, CO 81501

Alamo City Rivermen
P.O. Box 171194
San Antonio, TX 78217

Apalachee Canoe Club
P.O. Box 4027
Tallahassee, FL 32315
904-386-4984

Appalachian Mountain Club
5 Joy St.
Boston, MA 02108

Appalachian Paddling Enthusiasts
P.O. Box 60
Erwin, TN 37650

Arkansas Canoe Club
821 Akers Rd.
Hot Springs, AR 71902

Badger State Boating Society
2460 N. 80th St.
Wauwatosa, WI 53226
414-259-3204

Bayou City Whitewater Club
P.O. Box 980782
Houston, TX 77098

Bayou Haystackers Canoe Club
10525 Tams Dr.
Baton Rouge, LA 70815

Beartooth Paddlers Society
P.O. Box 20432
Billings, MT 59104

Blue Ridge Voyageurs
13102 Brahms Terrace
Silver Spring, MD 20904
301-890-8368

California Kayak Friends
14252 Culver Dr. A-199
Irvine, CA 92714
714-559-5076

Canoe Club of Greater Harrisburg
516 S. Lingle Ave.
Palmyra, PA 17078
717-838-8460

Canoe Cruisers Association
P.O. Box 15747
Chevy Chase, MD 20825

Carolina Canoe Club
P.O. Box 12932
Raleigh, NC 27605
919-834-1633

Cascaders
P.O. Box 580061
Minneapolis, MN 55458
612-452-8328

Central Georgia River Runners
P.O. Box 6563
Macon, GA 31208

Champaign Canoeing
c/o Ann LeClair
Brayton Park
Ossining, NY 10562-3201

Chicago Whitewater Association
1343 N. Portage
Palatine, IL 60067

Coastal Canoeists
P.O. Box 566
Richmond, VA 23204
804-231-0118

Colorado Whitewater Association
P.O. 4315
Englewood, CO 80155
303-430-4853

Conewago Canoe Club
c/o Figdores
2267 Willow Rd.
York, PA 17404
717-764-5834

Dallas Downriver Club
P.O. Box 595128
Dallas, TX 75359-5128
214-235-3356
214-497-1502

Florida Canoeing & Kayaking
  Association
P.O. Box 20892
West Palm Beach, FL 33416

Foothills Paddling Club
P.O. Box 6331
Greenville, SC 29606
803-653-8134

Garden State Canoe Club
Tony Baroni
R.R. 2, Box 8704-C
Milford, PA 18337
717-686-4717

Georgia Canoeing Association
P.O. Box 7023
Atlanta, GA 30357
404-421-9729

Gold Country Paddlers
637 Hovey Way
Roseville, CA 95678
916-783-3385

Greater Baltimore Canoe Club
P.O. Box 1841
Ellicott City, MD 21041

High Country River Rafters
P.O. Box 317
Wheat Ridge, CO 80034
303-935-6998

Housatonic Area Canoe and Kayak
Squad
104 Kent Rd.
Cornwall Bridge, CT 06754
203-672-0293

Houston Canoe Club
P.O. Box 925516
Houston, TX 77292-5516
713-467-8857

Idaho River Sports Canoe Club
1521 N. 13th St.
Boise, ID 83702
208-336-4844

Kayak and Canoe Club of New York
c/o Pierre De Rham
P.O. Box 195
Garrison, NY 10524
914- 424-3160

Keel Haulers Canoe Club
1649 Allen Dr.
Westlake, OH 44145
216-871-1758

Lansing Oar and Paddle Club
P.O. Box 26254
Lansing, MI 48909

Lehigh Valley Canoe Club
P.O. Box 4353
Bethlehem, PA 18018-0353
215-559-9595

Lower Columbia Canoe Club
1714 S.E. 52nd Ave.
Portland, OR 97215
503-649-3872

Mackinaw Canoe Club
R.R. 1, Box 314
Maroa, IL 61756

Merrimack Valley Paddlers
32 Tital Lane
Greenville, NH 03048
603-432-6870

Metropolitan Canoe & Kayak Club
P.O. Box 021868
Brooklyn, NY 11202-0040

Missouri Whitewater Association
325 DeBaliviere, #131
St. Louis, MO 63112
314-275-9964

Monocacy Canoe Clue
P.O. Box 1083
Frederick, MD 21702
301-831-9674

Monoco Canoe Club
304 Elton Adelphia Rd.
Freehold, NJ 07728
908-462-8743

North Texas River Runners
215 Lakeshore Dr.
Waxahachie, TX 75165
214-937-8835

Northwest Rafters Association
P.O. Box 19008
Portland, OR 97219
503-246-0386

Northwest Whitewater Association
P.O. Box 4941
Spokane, WA 99202
509-299-2777

Ohio Valley Whitewater Club
219 S. Walworth
Evansville, IN 47714
812-476-2185

Outdoor Adventure Club
P.O. Box 402
Dayton, OH 45404

Outdoor Club of South Jersey
P.O. Box 455
Cherry Hill, NJ 08003
609-931-0596

Paddle Trails Canoe Club
P.O. Box 24932
Seattle, WA 98124
206-784-7016

Philadelphia Canoe Club
4900 Ridge Ave.
Philadelphia, PA 19128
215-487-9674

Prairie State Canoeist
33312 Greentree Rd.
Wildwood, IL 60030
708-223-0642

Puget Sound Paddle Club
P.O. Box 22
Puyallup, WA 98371
206-841-3950

Rapids Riders
P.O. Box 13767
Dinkytown Station, MN 55414
612-933-4978

Rhode Island Canoe Association
70 Scott St.
Pawtucket, RI 02860
401-725-3344

Rocky Mountain Canoe Club
P.O. Box 280284
Lakewood, CO 80228
303-693-2109

Saukenuk Paddlers Canoe & Kayak Club
P.O. Box 1038
Moline, IL 61265

Sebago Canoe Club
Paerdegat Basin Foot of Ave. N
Brooklyn, NY 11236
718-241-3683

Seminole Canoe Club
4619 Ortega Farms Circle
Jacksonville, FL 32210
904-388-6734

Sequoia Paddling Club
P.O. Box 1164
Windsor, CA 95492

Smith River Valley Canoe Club
15 Cleveland Ave., #8
Martinsville, VA 24112
703-634-5600

Tennessee Scenic Rivers Association
P.O. Box 159041
Nashville, TN 37215

Three Rivers Paddling Club
c/o Barry Adams
811 Smokey Wood Dr.
Pittsburgh, PA 15218
412-242-4562

Toledo River Gang
3741 Wienwood
Toledo, OH 43623
419-874-9782

Triad River Runners
P.O. Box 24094
Winston-Salem, NC 27114
919-993-4500

Viking Canoe Club
P.O. Box 32263
Louisville, KY 40232
502-897-7056

Washington Recreational River Runners
P.O. Box 25048
Seattle, WA 98125
206-271-7655

Water Club
P.O. Box 3131
Grand Junction, CO 81502
303-464-7846

West Florida Canoe Club
P.O. Box 17203
Pensacola, FL 32522
904-433-3759

West Virginia Wildwater Association
P.O. Box 8413
South Charleston, WV 25303
304-744-0878

Western Carolina Paddlers
P.O. Box 8541
Asheville, NC 28814
704-258-8806

Western Waters Canoe Club
847 Gwen Dr.
Campbell, CA 95008

Whitewater Club of New Mexico
P.O. Box 3835
Albuquerque, NM 87190

Wildcat Canoe Club
P.O. Box 6232
Kokomo, IN 46904
317-457-7454

Williamette Kayak & Canoe Club
P.O. Box 1062
Corvallis, OR 97339
503-745-7055

Wilmington Trail Club
323 N. Shore Lane
Landsburg, PA 19350
215-274-2313

RIVER CONSERVATION ORGANIZATIONS

American Canoe Association
7432 Alban Station Blvd., Suite B-226
Springfield, VA 22150
703-451-0141

American Rivers
801 Pennsylvania Ave. S.E., Suite 303
Washington, DC 20003
202-547-6900

American Whitewater Affiliation
136 13th St. S.E.
Washington, DC 20003
202-546-3766

Friends of the River
909 12th St., Suite 207
Sacramento, CA 95814
916-442-3155

National Organization for River Sports
P.O. Box 6847
Colorado Springs, CO 80904
719-473-2466

The River Conservation Fund
323 Pennsylvania Ave. N.E.
Washington, DC 20003
202-547-6900

RIVER MANAGEMENT AGENCIES

Most of the popular boating rivers in this country flow through federal lands and are managed by the Forest Service, National Park Service, or Bureau of Land Management. Included below are the addresses of the regional offices of these agencies, as well as a list of specific rivers and their managing agencies, grouped according to state.

U.S. Forest Service
Department of Agriculture
Washington, DC 20250
Northern Region, Federal Building, Missoula, MT 59801
Southwestern Region, 517 Gold Ave., S.W., Albuquerque, NM 87102
California Region, 630 Sansome St., San Francisco, CA 94111
Intermountain Region, 324 25th St., Ogden, UT 84401
Pacific Northwest Region, 319 S.W. Pine St., P.O. Box 3623, Portland, OR 97208
Eastern Region, 633 W. Wisconsin Ave., Milwaukee, WI 53203
Southern Region, 1720 Peachtree Rd., N.W., Atlanta, GA 30309
Alaska Region, Federal Office Building, P.O. Box 1628, Juneau, AK 99502

National Park Service
Department of the Interior
Washington, DC 20240
Northeast Region, 143 S. Third St., Philadelphia, PA 19106
Southwest Region, P.O. Box 728, Santa Fe, NM 87501
Western Region, 450 Golden Gate Ave., Box 36036, San Francisco, CA 94102
Midwest Region, 1709 Jackson St., Omaha, NE 68102
Southeast Region, 3401 Whipple Ave., Atlanta, GA 30344

Bureau of Land Management
Department of the Interior
Washington, DC 20240
Alaska State Office, 555 Cordova St., Anchorage, AK 99510
Arizona State Office, 2400 Bank Center, Phoenix, AZ 85073
California State Office, Federal Building, 2800 Cottage Way, Sacramento, CA 95825
Colorado State Office, Room 700, Colorado State Bank Building, 1600 Broadway, Denver, CO 80202
Eastern States Office, 7981 Eastern Ave., Silver Spring, MD 20910

Montana State Office, Granite Tower,
   222 N. 32nd St., P.O. Box 30157,
   Billings, MT 30157
Nevada State Office, Federal Building,
   300 Booth St., Reno, NV 89509
New Mexico State Office, Federal Build-
   ing, South Federal Place, Santa Fe,
   NM 87501
Oregon State Office, University Club
   Building, 136 East South Temple,
   Salt Lake City, UT 84111
Wyoming State Office, 2515 Warren
   Ave., Cheyenne, WY 82001

ALASKA
Anchorage District Office
555 Cordova St.
Anchorage, AK 99501
Various Alaskan rivers

Glennallen Resource Area
Box 417
Glennallen, AK 99588
Delta, Gulkana

ARIZONA
Glen Canyon NRA
P.O. Box 1507
Page, AZ 86040
*Colorado (Glen Canyon Dam to Lees
Ferry), San Juan (below Mexican Hat)*

Grand Canyon National Park
P.O. Box 129
Grand Canyon, AZ 86023
Colorado (within park)

Havasu Resource Area
P.O. Box 685
Lake Havasu, AZ 86403
Lower Colorado (Parker to Davis)

Yuma Resource Area
2450 4th Ave.
Yuma, AZ 85364
Lower Colorado (Border to Parker)

ARKANSAS
Buffalo National River
P.O. Box 1173
Harrison, AR 72601
Buffalo

CALIFORNIA
Folsom District Office
63 Natoma St.
Folsom, CA 95630
*Stanislaus–American (North-South &
Middle Forks), Cosumnes, Mokelumne,
Merced, Yuba*

Klamath National Forest
1215 South Main
Yreka, CA 96097
Klamath, Salmon, Scott

Plumas National Forest
159 Lawrence Ave.
Quincy, CA 95971
Feather River–Middle Fork

Sequoia National Forest
800 Truxtun Ave.
Bakersfield, CA 93301
Kern

Shasta-Trinity National Forest
1615 Continental St.
Redding, CA 96001
*Sacramento, Trinity, Canyon Creek,
Hayfork Creek*

Sierra National Forest
P.O. Box 747
Mariposa, CA 95338
Merced

Sierra National Forest
Timmer Route
Sanger, CA 93657
Kings River

Six Rivers National Forest
710 E St.
Eureka, CA 95501
Smith, Mad, Eel

Stanislaus National Forest
Box 90
Groveland, CA 95321
Tuolumne

Tahoe National Forest
Nevada City, CA 95959
American–North Fork

COLORADO

Dinosaur National Monument
P.O. Box 210
Dinosaur, CO 86040
Green (within Monument), Yampa (within Monument)

Glenwood Springs Reservoir Area
Box 1009
Glenwood Springs, CO 81601
Colorado (Upper), Eagle

Routt National Forest
Walden, CO 80480
North Platte (North Gate Canyon)

IDAHO

Boise District Office
230 Collins Rd.
Boise, ID 83702
Owyee (above Three Forks), Bruneau, Jarbridge

Challis National Forest
Challis, ID 83226
Middle Fork of the Salmon

Clearwater National Forest
Kooskia, ID 83539
Lochsa, Clearwater–Middle Fork

Cottonwood Resource Area
Route 3
Cottonwood, ID 83522
Salmon (French Creek–Snake River), Snake (Zig-Zag Creek–Cougar Bar on the Idaho Side)

Idaho Panhandle National Forest
Sandpoint, ID 83864
Priest, St. Joe

Nez Perce National Forest
Kooskia, ID 83539
Selway, Clearwater–Middle Fork

Nez Perce National Forest
White Bird, ID 83554
Salmon (N. Fork to Riggins), Snake (Hells Canyon)

Payette National Forest
Snake (Hells Canyon)
Council, ID 83612
Salmon National Forest
North Fork ID 83466
Salmon (Salmon River Canyon)

Sawtooth NRA
Stanley, ID 83278
Salmon (Upper)

Targhee National Forest
Snake–Henrys Fork
Island Park, ID
Targhee National Forest
Rexburg, ID 83440
*Snake–South Fork (Grand Canyon,
Snake, Palisades–Heise)*

MISSOURI
Ozark National Scenic Riverways
Van Buren, MO 62965
Current, Jacks Fork

MONTANA
Bitterroot National Forest
Darby, MT 59829
Selway

Flathead National Forest
Kalispell, MT 59901
Three-Forks Flathead River

NEVADA
Carson City District Office
801 North Plaza
Carson City, NV 89701
Carson–East Fork

Lake Mead NRA
601 Nevada Highway
Boulder City, NV 89005
Colorado (within NRA)

Toiyabe National Forest
1536 S. Carson
Carson City, NV 89701
East Carson

OREGON
Prineville District
185 E. 4th St.
Prineville, OR 97753
Deschutes, John Day

Medford District
310 W. Sixth S.
Medford, OR 97501
Rogue

Siskiyou National Forest
Box 440
Grants Pass, OR 97526
Illinois

Vale District
Box 700
Vale, OR 97918
*Owyhee (Three Forks) to Owyhee
(Reservoir)*

Wallowa-Whitman National Forest
Federal Office Building
Box 907
Baker, OR 97814
Grande Ronde, Snake (Hells Canyon)

SOUTH CAROLINA
Sumter National Forest
Star Route
Walhalla, SC 29691
Chattooga

TEXAS
Big Bend National Park
Big Bend NP, TX 79834
Rio Grande (within park)

UTAH
Canyonlands National Park
446 S. Main
Moab, UT 84532
Colorado (within park), Green (within park)

Grand Resource Area
446 S. Main
Moab, UT 84532
Colorado (Westwater Canyon), Colorado (Rose Ranch to Castle Creek), Dolores (Utah part)

Flame Gorge NRA
Dutch John, UT 84032
Green (below dam)

North Vernal Resource Area
P.O. Box F
Vernal, UT 84078
Green (Little Hole to Park)

Price Resource Area
P.O. Drawer AB
Price, UT 84501
Green (Desolation–Gray Canyon)

San Juan Resource Area
P.O. Box 1327
Monticello, UT 84532
San Juan (above Mexican Hat)

WYOMING
Bridger-Teton National Forest
Afton, WY 83110
Greys

Grand Teton National Park
P.O. Box 67
Moose, WY 83012
Snake (within park)

big water: rivers with large volume and powerful hydraulics.

boulder garden: rapids densely strewn with boulders.

brace: a paddle stroke to prevent the kayak from flipping over.

breaking wave: a standing wave that falls upstream.

cfs: cubic feet per second; a measurement of the volume of water flowing past a given point per second.

chute: a narrow, constricted portion of the river.

cushion: see *pillow.*

draw stroke: sideways pull of the paddle toward the kayak.

eddy: an area in the river where the current either stops or moves upstream, opposite the main current; usually found below obstructions and on the inside of bends.

eddy line: the sharp boundary between two currents of different velocities or directions, usually marked by swirling water and bubbles.

feather: turn of the blade of a paddle horizontal to the water.

ferry: a maneuver for moving a boat laterally across the current, usually by paddling upstream or downstream at an angle.

gradient: the slope of a riverbed, usually expressed in the number of feet per mile the river drops.

haystack: a large, unstable standing wave.

hole: see *reversal.*

hypothermia: serious medical condition caused by the lowering of the body temperature; requires immediate first aid.

keeper: a large hole or reversal that can hold a swimmer for a long time.

lining: guiding the boat downstream from the shore with ropes to avoid running rapids.

pillow: a cushion of water that forms on the upstream side of rocks or other obstacles.

pool-and-drop: a river with intermittent rapids followed by long sections of calm water.

portage: to carry boats and equipment around the rapids.

put-in: the point at which a river trip is begun.

pry stroke: sideways push of the paddle away from the kayak.

reversal: an area of the river where the current turns upstream and revolves back on itself, forming a treacherous current requiring caution; often called hydraulics, stoppers, keepers, curlers, or holes.

riffle: shallow, gentle rapids.

roller: a big curling wave that falls back upstream on itself.

roostertail: a spray of water that explodes when it hits a rock or other obstacle.

scout: to examine a rapid from shore.

standing wave: a high wave caused by the slowing of the current.

stopper: a hole or breaking wave capable of stopping or flipping boats.

strainer: exposed rocks, usually on the outside of the bend, presenting a hazard to boaters.

sweeper: fallen tree or brush that lies in the path of the current.

tail wave: standing wave that forms at the base of a rapid.

take-out: the ending point of a river trip.

technical: a river with many obstacles, requiring constant maneuvering.

tongue: the smooth V of fast water found at the head of rapids, usually indicating the deepest and least obstructed channel.

undercut: a rock or ledge with water flowing underneath it.

wave train: a series of standing waves.

wrapping: the partial submersion that occurs when a kayak's upstream tube becomes lodged underwater against a boulder.

ACKNOWLEDGEMENTS

No book is published without the efforts of many other individuals besides the author, and this book is no exception. I am grateful to Judith Schnell and David Uhler of Stackpole Books for their kind works and enthusiastic support of the project. The editorial skills of Jane Devlin have greatly benefited the manuscript, and for that I am most appreciative.

I would like to thank my river colleagues over the years—too numerous to mention individually for fear of unintentionally forgetting someone—for their camaraderie on many a memorable journey downstream. Foremost among these is my wife Cherie, who would gladly follow me to any river in the world—and has. And to all my paddling buddies at the Nantahala Outdoor Center, I say thank you for your living inspiration of the old adage that "life is an adventure only for the adventurous."

For technical support on inflatable kayaks, I appreciate the consultations I had with Alan Hamilton and Greg Ramp of AIRE, who are also responsible for the splendid photography of Mark Lisk which graces the pages of this book.

And finally, the debt I owe to my family—to my parents and to my siblings Clark, Kathy, and Craig—knows no bounds—much like the sport this book hopes to celebrate.